PROBATE JURISDICTIONS:

WHERE TO LOOK FOR WILLS

FOURTH EDITION

Compiled by Jeremy Gibson

Federation of Family History Societies

First published by the **Federation of Family History Societies.**

Fourth edition, updated reprint with style alterations, published 1997 by
Federation of Family History Societies (Publications) Ltd., c/o The Benson Room,
Birmingham and Midland Institute, Margaret Street, Birmingham B3 3BS, England.

First edition, 1980.
Second edition, 1982, reprinted 1983.
Third edition, 1985, reprinted 1986, 1989.
Fourth edition, Copyright © J.S.W. Gibson, 1994, 1997.

ISBN 1 872094 69 4

Typeset in Aerial from disks prepared by Elizabeth Hampson and Jeremy Gibson.
Printed by Parchment (Oxford) Limited.

Cover illustration: detail of an engraving of the Hall of Doctors' Commons, where probate business was conducted for the Prerogative Court of Canterbury and several London courts of probate. For an informative and entertaining account of its workings, see *Hatred Pursued beyond the Grave: Tales of our Ancestors from the London Church Courts*, by Jane Cox, H.M.S.O. in association with the Public Record Office, 1993.

Acknowledgements

The information in this guide was initially largely based on that in my earlier book, *Wills and Where to Find Them* (1974). At that time I visited nearly all the probate record holding offices and received a great deal of help from archivists throughout the country. Since publication of this simplified version in 1980, updating has been a continuing process, repositories being regularly circulated (and specifically for this fourth edition) for news of the occasional change in location and the gratifyingly steady improvement in indexes and other finding aids. As always I have received a generous response. I would like once again to acknowledge my gratitude to all those archivists who so willingly help their enquirers, and I hope that this Guide will prove of use to them.

In this latest edition, my thanks are also due to Gervase Hood, who provided up-to-date information on continuing work at the Public Record Office on improving finding aids to the records of the Prerogative Court of Canterbury; to Don Steel, who suggested alterations and additions to the list of P.C.C. published abstracts and indexes; and to John Hebden, whose published calendar to Masham Peculier *(sic)* Court, with indexes to beneficiaries as well as testators, arrived in the nick of time for inclusion here. He has undertaken considerable research to endeavour to find other incidences of probate continuing to operate in courts other than P.C.C. during the interregnum.

The county maps showing probate jurisdictions are based on those in *Wills and Where to Find Them*, which themselves were loosely based on the excellent series of county parish maps published by The Institute of Heraldic and Genealogical Studies, Northgate, Canterbury. These have benefited countless genealogists, and serious researchers should acquire them for the counties in which they are interested.

At the request of my American distributers this edition does include a copyright notice, but, in recognition of the source of the information, record offices and family history societies are still welcome to reprint parts, with acknowledgment but no other requirement.

Finally it is my pleasure to thank Beth Hampson for her work retyping the Guide on to computer disk, but for which this new edition would have been much longer delayed.

Contents

Introduction

This guide to probate jurisdictions and their records is designed for the newcomer to local and family history. Its purpose is to suggest where to *start* looking for wills and their associated records.

For this reason, information on location of probate records before the mid-16th century is largely omitted. Wills before this date are in any case relatively rare; and anyone who has successfully researched back to this time, or who has decided to work on Tudor and earlier families, does not come into the category of 'beginner'. When users have exhausted the sources and indexes described in this guide, they too are no longer beginners. For further possible sources and for information on pre-Reformation jurisdictions, they should consult my earlier book, *Wills and Where to Find Them* (Phillimore and the British Record Society, 1974) or the even more detailed and authoritative *Wills and their Whereabouts* by Anthony J. Camp (4th edition, published by the author, 1974[1]). Although both are now out of print, copies of one or both are to be found in most reference libraries and record offices. The most important physical movement of probate records has been that occasioned by the lamented closure of the Chancery Lane Public Record Office building, which means that the P.C.C. records are now at Kew. However the registered copies, those normally seen by researchers, have long been primarily to be seen only on microfilm, and, as explained on pages 12-13, they are still available in this form as well in central London. Otherwise the only major movements of probate records since 1974 have been of Hereford diocesan records from the National Library of Wales to Hereford, of Berkshire archdeaconry and Oxford consistory and archdeaconry records from the Bodleian to the Berkshire Record Office and Oxfordshire Archives (Office) respectively, of Ely consistory and archdeaconry records from Cambridge University Library to the Cambridge branch of the Cambridgeshire Record Office, and of Middlesex records to London Metropolitan Archives (formerly the Greater London Record Office). The developments of the past two decades are indicated in this Guide.

As this is a guide to records of the nineteenth and earlier centuries, it has been logical to arrange it according to the counties as they existed before local government reorganisation in 1974. For the same reason local record offices are still maintained for counties, such as Huntingdon, which have been absorbed into larger administrative areas.

Wills since 1858

The crucial date for testamentary research in England and Wales is 1858, when the present centralised system was introduced. From this date, copies of all wills and letters of administration ('admons.', for people not leaving wills) are to be found at the Principal Registry of the Family Division, Somerset House, Strand, in central

---

[1] This builds on Camp's own earlier (third) edition, incorporating information provided by archivists nationwide, published by Phillimore for the Society of Genealogists in 1963, the second edition having been revised in 1952 by Helen Thacker from the original book by B.G. Bouwens (1939), both also published by the Society; Bouwens' acknowledges his sources of various Government *Command Papers*, 1828-1845 and a Stationery Office *Index of Courts*, 1862; he died in 1943 so his copyright, purchased by Camp from his heirs, has now expired; nevertheless any unauthorised publication of material which might be construed as having come from *Wills and their Whereabouts* may be subject to legal proceedings.

London. However, printed indexes (or the microfiche edition) to these are often held locally. Locations are given under each county heading and on page 11. Registered copies of wills proved at district registries are now often held by local record offices, and such holdings are also shown under individual counties. In some cases original wills have been retained by the district registries (and are so indicated), but many collections have been deposited with the Public Record Office and are now at Hayes.

Before 1858

Before 1858, probate was handled by ecclesiastical courts, with jurisdiction in archdeaconries, dioceses of bishops (consistory courts) and provinces of the archbishops of Canterbury and York (prerogative courts, usually abbreviated to P.C.C. and P.C.Y.); there were also areas exempt from archdiaconal and episcopal jurisdiction, known as 'peculiars'. Probate records of P.C.C. are in the Public Record Office at Kew (but wills and admons. also available on microfilm in central London); for fuller details of indexes, etc, see page 12. Wills and admons. of the important and the wealthy, the nobility, gentry, landowners, prosperous merchants and tradesmen, and those that died overseas, are most likely to be found in this collection; but use of the court was by no means confined to such classes, so indexes to P.C.C. should still be searched however humble a testator may be thought to be.

P.C.C. had jurisdiction throughout England and Wales, though wills of testators from counties in the northern province of York (Cheshire, Cumberland, Durham, Flint (southern detachment), Lancashire, Northumberland, Nottinghamshire, Westmorland and Yorkshire) are more likely to be found in P.C.Y., see page 56.

Apart from P.C.C. and P.C.Y. probate records for any particular county in England are likely to be found at the county record office (acting as diocesan record office). The main exceptions are:

Derbyshire: Joint Record Office, Lichfield.
Durham: Durham University Library (Archives and Special Collections).
London and Middlesex: mainly at Guildhall Library and London Metropolitan Archives (formerly Greater London Record Office).
Monmouthshire: National Library of Wales.
Rutland: Northamptonshire Record Office.
Shropshire: split between Hereford, Lichfield and the National Library of Wales.
Staffordshire: Joint Record Office, Lichfield.
Surrey: London Metropolitan Archives (formerly G.L.R.O.).
Warwickshire: split between Lichfield and Worcester.
Westmorland: split between Cumbria R.O., Carlisle and Lancashire R.O., Preston.
Yorkshire: mainly at the Borthwick Institute, York, some at Leeds District Archives.
Wales: National Library of Wales.

Although the jurisdiction of the ecclesiastical courts was by archdeaconries and dioceses, these usually coincided with county boundaries and so make identification of court much easier than may at first appear. There are of course numerous exceptions, some affecting large or populous areas, many the occasional parish. It is the purpose of this guide to lead its users to the correct indexes and record offices both for places which fall within the expected jurisdictions and for those that are the exceptions.

Probate Documents and Procedures

Although there was a great variety of courts in which wills were proved the types of document produced by the process are basically the same whichever court was responsible. The main record is obviously the will, supplemented by an inventory of the deceased's goods and by grants of probate and administration.

Wills survive in two forms: the originals which were filed away after being exhibited in the probate court and the registered copy, being a transcription of the will made at the time of probate and bound into a large volume.

When a will is exhibited in the probate court and found to be valid a grant of probate is made to the executors. The grant is similar to the administration bond, which is taken out by a person or persons who are to administer the goods of someone who has died intestate. Both documents survive, like wills, in two forms. Firstly a record of the grant of probate or administration is made in the probate act books, the details noted generally including the name, condition (i.e. occupation - blacksmith, innholder, gent., etc.) and place of residence of the deceased, with similar information about the executors/administrators, and a note of their relationship, if any, to the deceased. Secondly, there are the bonds, which are signed by the executors/administrators and, as well as including the above information, also give the sum of money the executors/administrators are bound to forfeit if they do not fulfil their task to the satisfaction of the court. This sum is normally about twice the value of the deceased's personal estate. The bonds are filed away with the original wills.

When a person dies leaving children to be cared for the executors/administrators have to enter into tuition or curation bonds, which record the same information as the administration bond but, since they are bonds to look after the deceased's children rather than to administer his estate, they record the names of the children concerned. Again, these bonds survive in two forms. There are the originals, filed away with the wills and administration bonds and there are registered copies, which can either be in the probate act books or in a volume specifically kept for that purpose.

Inventories are lists of the deceased's goods and chattels exhibited in the probate court. In theory an inventory should accompany each will or grant of administration, but in practise, as might be expected, this is not always the case. Their survival varies from diocese to diocese and even from probate court to probate court within a single diocese. For the Prerogative Court of Canterbury they only survive in any quantity between 1661 and c.1700, but many local courts have good collections for the later sixteenth and the seventeenth centuries. In general later inventories are less informative and they die out in the eighteenth century.

[These notes on probate procedures and documents are based, by kind permission of the Borthwick Institute of Historical Research, on the Institute's *Guide to Genealogical Sources*, by C.C. Webb, 1981. For a more recent and much fuller description, see *An Introduction to ... Affection Defying the Power of Death: Wills, Probate and Death Duty Records*, by Jane Cox, F.F.H.S., 1993.]

Glossary

Account: The 'true and just account' which executors or administrators sometimes had to render.

Act: The endorsement on a will indicating probate had been granted, the record of a grant in an act book.

Act Book: A day-by-day account of the official grants of probate wills, letters of administration (admon.), and other testamentary business.

Administration, Letters of (usually abbreviated to Admon.) A grant to the next-of-kin (or some other person or persons) who applied to administer the property of an intestate.

Administration (Letters of) with Will annexed: A grant, usually to the next-of-kin, when the will did not specify any executors or they were unable to act, or renounced, or had died. The will is then attached to the admon. bond. Sometimes filed under admons. instead of wills.

Administrator: A man vested with the right to administer an estate, normally, in the case of an intestate, the next-of-kin; but one might be appointed when the executor, or next-of-kin, was a minor. An **Administratrix** was a woman.

Admon.: See **Administration, Letters of**.

Archdeaconry: Normally the lowest of the ecclesiastical courts with testamentary jurisdiction. In larger dioceses there might be several, often co-terminous with counties (*cf.* Berkshire in the diocese of Salisbury), whilst just one might cover the whole of a smaller diocese (*cf.* Oxford). It was not unusual for the bishop's consistory court to appropriate this jurisdiction (*cf.* Lichfield), or for a commissary to be appointed for an archdeaconry (*cf.* Buckingham in the diocese of Lincoln.

Bona Notabilia: A Latin term meaning considerable goods, technically worth £5 and more. When the deceased had *bona notabilia* in more than one jurisdiction, a will should have been proved in a superior court.

Bond: A signed and witnessed obligation, the conditions of which might include the proving of a will, administration of an intestate's estate, rendering an account or inventory, or guardianship of a minor.

Calendar: In this guide, this generally implies an index, chronological within initial letter, normally contemporary with the records. A modern fully alphabetical index is to be preferred.

Caveat: A warning notice that a will is to be disputed.

Citation: A summons to appear before a court.

Commissariot: In Scotland the district within the jurisdiction of a commissary court. In 1823 the old districts were abolished, and most commissariots thereafter coincided with the old sheriffdoms (counties) and the sheriff court districts, with which they were merged in 1876. See also **Sheriffdom** and **Sheriff Court**.

Commissary: A person who held authority or a commission to exercise jurisdiction on behalf of an archbishop, bishop or other dignitary; the title continued to be used in Scotland in spite of the abolition of episcopal authority.

Commissary Court: A court acting with delegated powers from the bishop, normally as a consistory court but in one archdeaconry only - in contrast to an archdeaconry court which was subject to the archdeacon. In Scotland, one of the courts which took over the jurisdiction of the pre-reformation church courts.

Confirmation: In Scotland, the completion of the probate of a testament by the executors.

Consistory Court: The bishop's ecclesiastical court, with superior jurisdiction to an archdeaconry court. Theoretically wills of testators with 'bona notabilia' in two archdeaconries within the same diocese would be proved in the consistory court, and often the wills of clergy were reserved to it. In many dioceses it displaced the archdeaconry court entirely (*cf.* Lichfield), or had jurisdiction over certain parishes exempt from the archdeacon's jurisdiction (*cf.* Canterbury). In large dioceses powers were often delegated from the consistory court of the diocese to commissary courts acting in different archdeaconries archdeaconries (*cf.* Buckingham in the diocese of Lincoln). The consistory court would normally have jurisdiction during periodic visitations of the bishop to different archdeaconries, when the archdeaconry court would be inhibited (see **Inhibition**).

Curation: Guardianship over orphaned minors, under 21 but over 14 (boys) or 12 (girls). See also **Tuition**.

Dean (and Chapter): Clergy who were members of a cathedral chapter, often with peculiar jurisdiction over parishes in the patronage of that cathedral.

Diocese: The district over which a bishop has authority.

Executor (often abbreviated to **Exor.**): A man appointed by the testator to see that the provisions of a will are carried out. An executrix is a woman.

Grant: Approval of the submission of the executor or administrator, denoting probate or letters of administration.

Guardianship: See **Curation** and **Tuition**.

Honour: See **Manor**.

Inhibition: The period during the visitation of a bishop to an archdeaconry, when the archdeacon's court would be closed and probate business conducted in the consistory court. In theory the visitation of an archbishop to a diocese would have the same effect on a consistory court, but in post-medieval times this was likely to be 'pro forma' only. Some peculiars were entirely exempt from visitation and inhibition, others were subject to visitation by a dean or a dean and chapter. Visitations would normally last several months at intervals of several years.

Intestate: A person who died without making a will.

Inventory: A list of personal and household goods left by the deceased, with their appraised value. Occupation was usually given, or can be inferred from tools of trade. They were common in the later 16th and 17th centuries, but became much less detailed and frequent in the 18th century; except in Scotland where they continued to a much later date.

Jurisdiction: The area over which a court claimed the right to grant probate or letters of administration. Peculiars within this area would be exempt from the jurisdiction of the court concerned.

Letters of Administration: See **Administration**.

Liberty: See **Manor**.

Manor: Occasional manorial courts had peculiar or exempt jurisdiction over a parish or part of a parish. An **Honour** (*cf.* Knaresborough, Yorks.) or **Liberty** (*cf.* Frampton, Dorset) might be a group of manors with such exempt jurisdiction.

Nuncupative Will: A will made orally, normally by a testator on his deathbed, written down and sworn to by witnesses, but not signed by the deceased.

Peculiar (Testamentary): A parish or group of parishes, not necessarily adjacent or even in the same district or county, which were usually exempt from the testamentary jurisdiction of the archdeaconry and often the consistory court. Ecclesiastical peculiars were often subject to a dean or dean and chapter, though they might be administered by a locally appointed official; a bishop's peculiar might be administered by the consistory court; a number were royal or archbishop's peculiars, usually locally administered; and there were some lay, manorial or collegiate, peculiars. See also **Inhibition**.

Personalty: Personal property (goods, chattels, credits, etc.) as opposed to **real property**. In Scotland, until 1868, and in the Channel Islands only personalty (moveable property) could be bequeathed, and a document so excluding realty is technically known as a testament.

Prebend: So far as testamentary matters are concerned, this was a type of ecclesiastical peculiar, in the jurisdiction of a prebendary, who was appointed by the dean and chapter of a cathedral; accordingly it was usually subject to their visitation and inhibition.

Prerogative Court: See **Province**.

Probate: Evidence that a will has been accepted and that the executor has been granted permission to carry out its provisions.

Proved: A will has been proved when probate has been granted.

Province: The dioceses over which an archbishop has authority, i.e., before 1858, in England and Wales, the provinces of Canterbury and York, and in Ireland, the province of Armagh. The **prerogative courts courts** of the archbishops had superior jurisdiction to all others, and Canterbury was superior to York.

Realty, Real Property, Real Estate: Property or interests in land, as opposed to personalty. In Scotland, until 1868, and in the Channel Islands, realty (heritable property) could not be bequeathed, and in England there were certain limitations on its bequest, so that it does not always appear in wills.

Registers and Registered Wills: Volumes of copy wills, made at the time of probate. It is these the searcher will normally see, though sometimes only original wills are available. At times only the registered copies survive. These are not to be confused with archbishops' and bishops' registers, which record their provincial and diocesan activities, but also include occasional wills, particularly in medieval times.

Renunciation: When an executor declines to apply for probate.

Sede Vacante: See **Vacancy**.

See: Often used as a synonym for diocese, though technically the seat of the bishop or the diocesan centre.

Sentences: The final judgement on a disputed will, often entered in an act book.

Sheriff Court: In Scotland, since 1876 the court with testamentary jurisdiction over anyone dying within its district, usually a county or part of a county. There are several such districts in each modern sheriffdom. Its official, the sheriff clerk, has custody of current testamentary records and also often of the 1823-1876 records of the commissariot court of the former sheriffdom, which the modern sheriff court district has replaced.

Sheriffdom: In Scotland, an administrative area, generally in the mid-19th century coinciding with a county, which between 1823 and 1876 acted as a commissariot district. In more recent years their number has been reduced and each now incorporates several counties and sheriff court districts. See also **Commissariot**.

Surrogate: A deputy appointed by the ecclesiastical court to deal with testamentary and other matters.

Testament: Normally a synonym for a **will**, but technically a document which excludes **realty** (heritable property), as in Scotland and the Channel Islands.

Testator: A man who has made a will. A testatrix is a woman.

Tuition: Guardianship over orphaned minors, under 15 (boys) or 13 (girls). See also **Curation**.

Vacancy: A break in the official business of the court on the death or translation of the bishop or other chief official. The court might be closed and business carried on in another court, but often this was 'pro forma' only, i.e. the same actual officials carried on, powers from the alternative court being delegated to them.

Warrants (of testaments): In Scotland, normally the drafts from which the entries in the register were made up, but occasionally including original wills.

Will: A written statement by which a person regulates the disposition of property and rights after his or her death, normally signed and witnessed. See also **Testament**.

Abbreviations

Admon.	Letters of Administration
BRS	*British Record Society*
C19	19th century
Inv.	Inventory
MS	Manuscript
SofG or *SG*	*Society of Genealogists*
SRS	*Scottish Record Society*
TS	Typescript

ENGLAND and WALES

Since 1858: A centralised system for probate came into operation in England and Wales on 12 January 1858, with a principal probate registry in London and a chain of district probate registries in important centres. A similar system came into operation in Ireland at the same date (see page 70) and to an extent in Scotland in 1876 (see page 68). Testamentary matters for the Channel Islands and the Isle of Man are still in the jurisdiction of local courts.

In England and Wales a consolidated Index of Grants of probate and letters of administration within the year has been printed annually. Before 1870, admons. were listed separately at the end of volumes.

These indexes may be consulted without charge at the

> **Principal Registry of the Family Division,**
> *Somerset House, Strand, London WC2R 1LP,*
> (formerly known as the Principal Probate Registry).

Copies of these annual indexes were sent to district probate registries, but those over 50 years old have in most cases been transferred to local record offices or libraries. Their present locations are listed right. In addition, the indexes up to 1935 have been produced in a microfiche edtion by the Hampshire Record Office, so are now probably much more widely available. They can be a useful short cut to finding the death of an adult even if the will is not immediately available.

There are copies of all these wills and admons. since 1858 at Somerset House. These may be consulted on payment of a small fee. Photocopies are obtainable from the Probate Sub-Registry, Duncombe Place, York YO1 2EA. Records over one hundred years old may be consulted without charge by holders of a search permit, obtainable on prior application to the Record Keeper at Somerset House.

When probate was taken out at a district probate registry, that registry retained the original will and made a registered copy (in a bound volume) before forwarding a further copy to the Principal Registry. These registered copies have been mostly deposited at local record offices. In some cases district registries still retain the original wills, but often they have been sent to a Public Record Office out-repository (to consult these at the P.R.O., a week's notice is necessary). Until 1926 individual district probate registries only had jurisdiction in their own districts, in general coinciding with the counties in which they lay. There were none in the home counties. Present location of registered copies and originals if still held locally is given under each county.

Avon: Bristol Record Office, 1858-1900.
Beds.: County Record Office, 1901-1935
Cambs.: County Record Office (Cambs C.C.), Cambridge, 1858-1934.
Cheshire: Cheshire Record Office, 1858-1929.
Cornwall: Bodmin Sub-Registry, Bodmin, for eventual transfer to the Cornwall Record Office, Truro.
Cumbria: Cumbria Record Office, Carlisle, 1858-1928.
Devon: Exeter Sub-Registry, Exeter.
Glos.: Gloucestershire Record Office, 1858-1929.
Gtr. Manchester: Greater Manchester Record Office, Manchester.
Hants.: Hampshire Record Office, Winchester 1858-1932.
Lancs.: Lancashire Record Office, Preston 1858-1928.
Leics.: Leicestershire Record Office, 1858-1890 (not in main record office, prior notice required); Leicester Probate Registry, Leicester.
Lincs: Lincolnshire Archives Office, 1858-1933.
Merseyside: Liverpool Record Office, Liverpool, 1858-1928.
Norfolk: Norwich Local Studies Library, 1858-1937.
Northants.: *see* Cambridgeshire.
Notts.: Nottinghamshire Record Office, 1858-1928.
Oxon.: Bodleian Library, Oxford (Lower Reading Room, Radcliffe Camera, on open shelves - readers ticket necessary, daily charge).
East Sussex: East Sussex Record Office, Lewes 1858-1928.
West Midlands: Birmingham Reference Library (Archives Dept.), 1858-1937.
North Yorks.: York Sub-Registry, York .
South Yorks.: Sheffield Record Office, 52 Shoreham Street, Sheffield, 1858-1928 (prior notice required; no public access, short searches undertaken by staff).
West Yorks.: West Yorkshire County Record Office, Wakefield, 1858-1928.
Clwyd: Clwyd Record Office, Ruthin, 1858-1928.
Dyfed: National Library of Wales, Aberystwyth, 1858-1972.
Dyfed Archives, Carmarthen, 1858-1928.
Glamorgan: Glamorgan Record Office, Cardiff, 1858-1928 (from LLandaff).
Gwynedd: Gwynedd Archives Service, Caernarfon, 1858-1929 (from Bangor).

District registries were also issued with a 16-volume set index to wills and admons. in **P.C.C., 1853-1858**. Copies of this are now located as below. This index is included in the microfiche edition published by Hampshire Record Office.

Cambs. County Record Office, Cambridge.
Exeter Sub-Registry.
Hampshire Record Office.
Kent Archives Office, Maidstone.
Leicestershire Record Office (prior notice required).
Lincolnshire Archives Office.
Birmingham Reference Library (Archives Department).
Liverpool Record Office.
London: Public Record Office [PROB 12/272-288] (hard copy print at Family Records Centre; film at Kew).
Norwich Central Library (Local Studies).
Nottinghamshire Record Office.
Oxford, Bodleian Library.
East Sussex Record Office, Lewes.
York Sub-Registry.
Sheffield Record Office (see above).
Clwyd Record Office, Ruthin.
Dyfed: National Library of Wales. Aberystwyth.
Gwynedd Archives Service, Caernarfon.

ENGLAND AND WALES

Before 1858: As explained in the Introduction, probate records of the wealthy and important, particularly those with goods and property in more than one diocese, are likely to be found in the Prerogative Court of the archbishop rather than in the local consistory, archdeaconry or peculiar courts held in the diocesan record offices. It is emphasised that these were not confined to such classes, and indexes to the higher courts are always worth searching, especially in the case of soldiers, seamen, and other persons dying overseas, whatever standing the testator may be thought to have had.

The most important was the **Prerogative Court of Canterbury (P.C.C.)**. This claimed over-riding jurisdiction in England and Wales, though few testators from the northern province of York in fact occur: for those counties (Cheshire, Cumberland, Durham, Flint (southern detachment), Lancashire, Northumberland, Nottinghamshire, Westmorland and Yorkshire) see the Prerogative Court of York (P.C.Y.) (page 56).

Wills of those dying overseas were also usually proved in P.C.C. However they are to be found in the records of other courts, particularly the London courts (page 36).

Records of **P.C.C.** are in the

> **Public Record Office,** Ruskin Avenue, Kew, Richmond, Surrey TW9 4DU

lettercode PROB. Microfilm of PROB 11 (registered wills) and PROB 6 (administration act books) are made available both at Kew and in central London at the

> **Family Records Centre (P.R.O.),** 1 Myddelton Street, London EC1R 1VW.

Leaflet *Probate Records*, available. A Readers' ticket should be obtained beforehand. On the open shelves are the many volumes of printed or modern indexes (wills to 1800, admons to 1660); unsuperseded contemporary MS calendars to 1852 or copies of them [PROB 12/38-70, 120-271]; official printed index, 1853-1858 (10 January) [PROB 272-288]. Published and typescript indexes are generally duplicated on both sites.

The individual will registers were originally allocated names (usually based on that of some significant testator). These are quoted in many of the older printed indexes. Once a will is located, with its year and number, the PROB 11 class list (of which there are copies on the shelves) must be consulted to identify the P.R.O. reference for the will register. This will enable you to identify the microfilm you need. The number given in the index or calendar is that allocated to each gathering of 16 pages in the bound volumes, not to the later rubber stamped foliation numbers, so when spinning through the microfilm, the relatively occasional quire numbers have to be looked for.

Wills in the records of the P.C.C. date from 1383 and admons from 1559. The printed indexes to these are detailed below. During the Interregnum (1653-1660) this court, in the form of a civil institution, had sole jurisdiction in England and Wales, and effectively for much of the preceding ten years from the outbreak of the Civil War.

Indexes to P.C.C. Wills (printed unless shown otherwise):

1383-1558 *BRS 10* and *11*.
1558-1583 *BRS 18*.
1584-1604 *BRS 25*.
1605-1619 *BRS 43*.
1620 *Register Soame*, abstracts, by J.H. Lea, 1904.
1620-1624 *Year Books of Probates: Probates and Sentences* by J. and G.F..Matthews, 1914 (this contains additional references to *BRS 44*).
1620-1629 *BRS 44*.
1630 *Register Scroope*, abstracts, by J.H. Morrison, with index to stray names.
1630-1639 *Sentences and Complete Index Nominum* (surnames only) J. and G.F. Matthews, 1907; also indexes of stray names 1640-44, 1645-49, 1650-51, 1652-53.
1630-1655 *Year Books of Probate* by J. and G.F. Matthews vols. *1-8*, 1902-27. *Note.* 1655 is A-M only (N-Z never published).
The Matthews volumes are *very* confusingly numbered.
1630-1652 TS indexes to testators (full names) by P. Boyd at *SofG*.
1651 MS abstracts of *Register Grey*, by Mrs A. Rowan, 15 vols., at *SofG*.
1653-1656 *BRS 54*.
Jan.1657/8-June 1658 *Register Wootton* by W.Brigg, 7 vols.
1657-1660 *BRS 61*.
1661-1670 *Wills, Sentences and Probate Acts*. J.H. Morrison, 1935.
1671-1675 *BRS 67*.
1676-1685 *BRS 71*.
1686-1693 *BRS 77*.
1694-1700 *BRS 80*.
1701-1749 Index by the Friends of the Public Record Office.
1750 *Register Greenly*, by G. Sherwood, a list of all persons named, arranged in 8 groups, topographically - not indexed (copy at *Soc. of Gen.*, but not at P.R.O.).
1750-1800 *Index to Wills proved in P.C.C.*, ed. A.J. Camp, Society of Genealogists, 6 vols., 1976-92.
1807-1845 *An Index to the Bank of England will abstracts, 1808-1845*, Society of Genealogists, 1991, provides a partial printed source of information.

1853-1858 (10 Jan.) Consolidated index, with admons, in 16 vols. For location of other copies see page 12, column 1; also published on microfiche by Hampshire Record Office.

For all of the period 1801-1852 it is otherwise necessary to consult the contemporary MS calendars at the P.R.O. However, for 1796-1903, see also the Death Duty Registers and Indexes, below.

Printed **indexes to P.C.C. admons.**:
1559-1580 *Administrations in P.C.C.*, by R.M. Glencross, 2 vols., 1912-1917. TS corrigenda at P.R.O. MS index of places, 1559-1571 at SofG.
1581-1595 *BRS 76*
1596-1608 *BRS 81*
1609-1619 *BRS 83*
1620-1630 *Letters of Administration*, by J.H. Morrison. 1934/5.
1631-1648 *BRS 100*
1649-1654 *BRS 68*
1655-1660 *BRS 72, 74, 75*.

There are ts indexes to 1661 (A to Sweetinge only) and to 1663-64. The FPRO index covers both wills and admons, 1701-1749. The Soc. of Gen. has a card index to PCC admons 1750-1800. Otherwise it is necessary to consult the contemporary MS calendars, except 1853-1858, see above.

Inventories in P.C.C. rarely survive except for the period 1661 to early 18th century. The very few pre-1661 (c.825) are listed at the P.R.O. [PROB.2]. Indexes to places, people, trades.

1661 to early C18 (6,180) ('miscellaneous') inventories in PROB.5, printed index *(List & Index Soc. 149*, to 1-6105 only; full list and index to 6106-6180 at P.R.O.).
1661 to early C18 (26,061) ('engrossed') inventories in PROB.4, TS list and slip index.
1718-1760 (and a few to 1782) (5,500) *(List & Index Soc. 85, 86*, incomplete*)*, revised lists and index at P.R.O.

There are also inventories in PROB 28 (1642-1722), PROB 31 (1722-1858), PROB 32 (1661-1723), PROB 36 (1653-1721), and PROB 37 (1783-1858).

For further information see *Wills and Other Probate Records*, by Miriam Scott (P.R.O., 1997, £5.99).

There were two courts of appeal from P.C.C.: the P.R.O. has the records of **The High Court of Delegates**, to which there is a printed index, wills and admons., 1651-1857 (550) [in DEL 9, 10] in *The Genealogist, 11* and *12*. Its functions were taken over by the Judicial Committee of the Privy Council in 1832 [PCAP 1-5].

Records of the second court of appeal from P.C.C., the **Court of Arches**, are at Lambeth Palace Library, London. There is a printed index to wills, admons and invs (in disputed cases), 1660-1857 *(BRS 85)*.

Also at the P.R.O. are the registers to the taxes collectively known as **Death Duties** [IR 26], another useful finding aid for those trying to locate the court in which a will or admon was recorded. They cover the years **1796** to **1903**. The registers and the indexes [IR 27] to them have largely been microfilmed, and these films are on open access, also available in central London. Unfilmed pieces in IR 26 are produced at Kew (three days notice required).

They consist of abstracts of most, but by no means all, wills and admons, which had to be deposited at the Legacy Duty Department of the Stamp Office. For some areas they do not start until after 1800.

The indexes for the whole period are particularly valuable. Prior to 1812 they are arranged in three groups: P.C.C. wills, P.C.C. admons, and 'Country Courts', wills and admons, arranged court by court.

From 1812 the grouping alters and becomes vastly more useful, as all wills are indexed in one consolidated series, whatever the court. P.C.C. admons remain in a separate series; and all admons from the 'Country Courts' are indexed in a third (consolidated) series. They are confusingly laid out and before attempting to use them the P.R.O. leaflet **34** Death Duty Registers and the introductory notes to the IR 26 and IR 27 class lists are essential reading.

See also Wills, Inventories and Death Duties: A Provisional Guide, by Jane Cox (P.R.O., 1988, now o.p.).

Wills in the Public Record Office

As well as possessing numerous small collections of original or copy wills, the Public Record Office also contains some very large ones, quite apart from the P.C.C. and Stamp Office records mentioned above. Most of these probably appear in P.C.C. or some other court. The publication List of Wills, Admons, etc., in the Public Record Office (Magna Charta Book Co. 1968) is based on an unrevised TS in the Family Records Centre dated 1932, and as a survey is both out of date and incomplete. See Miriam Scott's Wills and Other Probate Records and Jane Cox's Wills, Inventories and Death Duties for otehr possible sources.

Society of Genealogists, 14 Charterhouse Buildings, Goswell Road, London EC1M 7BA.

The Society in its unique library and MSS collections includes virtually all printed indexes to wills and admons, much TS and MS material (including indexes), and thousands of abstracts. Of particular importance is its collection of microfilms of calendars of wills and admons - these were microfilmed by the Church of Jesus Christ of Latter-Day Saints some years ago, so usually are of 19th century and earlier indexes and calendars, which may well have been superseded since. Nevertheless they are useful for those able to get to London more easily than to the local record offices concerned.

The Society's collection in general is described definitively in Will Indexes and Other Probate Material in the Library of the Society of Genealogists (Library Sources No. **8**), by Nicholas Newington-Irving, 1996, so all but the barest details, under relevant counties, are omitted in this work.

BEDFORDSHIRE

Since 1858: Probate records for England and Wales are at the *Principal Registry of the Family Division, Somerset House, Strand, London WC2R 1LP*. Indexes to these are held locally at the *Beds. R.O.*, 1900-1935 only; see also page 11.

Registered copy wills for Bedfordshire 1858-1930 are deposited at the *Northamptonshire Record Office* and are indexed to 1908.

Before 1858: Bedfordshire formed the archdeaconry of Bedford in the diocese of Lincoln and province of Canterbury.

Apart from P.C.C. (see page 12 and below), virtually all probate records for the whole county are at the

Bedfordshire Record Office, Bedford.

One index covers the **Archdeaconry of Bedford** and the two **Peculiars of Biggleswade** and **Leighton Buzzard**. Wills **1480-1857**, admons **1670-1857**; Biggleswade Peculiar from 1720 only. Leighton Buzzard Peculiar from 1701 only. This is published in two volumes (*BRS **104, 105***). Its introduction lists publications in which early Beds. wills have appeared.

Exception:
Everton, in Archdeaconry of Huntingdon, see p. 31.

Note. Although in the Diocese of Lincoln, consistory powers were delegated to the local Bedford court.

Prerogative Court of Canterbury
The *Beds. R.O.* has copies of most P.C.C. wills for Beds. people up to 1700 (and some P.C.C. invs), all card indexed. See also *B.H.R.S. **58***, below.

Printed Sources
*Genealogia Bedfordiensis, **1538-1700*** by F.A. Blaydes has numerous abstracts of Beds. wills arranged by parish.

Beds. wills **1480-1528** (from Archdeaconry Court) are abstracted in *Beds. Hist. Rec. Soc. **37** and **45***.

*Bedfordshire Wills proved in the P.C.C. **1383-1548***, ed. Margaret McGregor (*Beds. Hist. Record Soc. **58***). Abstracts.

*Inventories of Bedfordshire Houses, 1714-1830, Beds. Hist. Rec. Soc. **74*** (only 18, mainly from estate collections rather than probate).

Places in Bedfordshire outside the jurisdiction of the archdeaconry (see map):
1. Everton (archdeaconry of Huntingdon)
2. Peculiar of Biggleswade
3. Peculiar of Leighton Buzzard:
   Leighton Buzzard and its former hamlets of
   Billington
   Eggington
   Heath and Reach
   Stanbridge

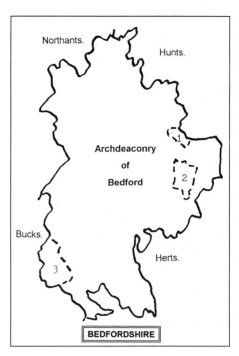

BEDFORDSHIRE

BERKSHIRE
(north-western Vale of the White Horse now in Oxfordshire)

Since 1858: Probate records for England and Wales are at the *Principal Registry of the Family Division, Somerset House, Strand, London WC2R 1LP*. Indexes to these to 1928 are held locally at the *Bodleian Library, Oxford (Radcliffe Camera, Lower Reading Room)*, and on microfiche at the *Centre for Oxfordshire Studies, Oxford Central Library*.

Before 1858: Berkshire formed the archdeaconry of Berkshire in the diocese of Salisbury and province of Canterbury. In 1836 the archdeaconry was transferred to the diocese of Oxford.

The *Society of Genealogists* has, in the *Snell collection*, a MS list of Berkshire wills in **P.C.C. 1631-1807** (vols. **16** and **21**) with complete abstracts **1391-1737** (in 15 volumes) and a 25 volume index of names and places.

Apart from P.C.C. (see page 12), most probate records for the county are now at the *Berkshire Record Office*; but there are also some at the *Wiltshire Record Office; Oxfordshire Archives;* and a few at *Windsor Castle*.

15

Berkshire, continued

Records of the **Archdeaconry of Berkshire** (which covered all parishes except those listed right) are now at the

> **Berkshire Record Office,** Reading.

There are printed indexes to these **Berkshire Archdeaconry** wills and admons **1508-1652** *(BRS 8* and *Oxford Hist. Soc. 23)* and to all probate records **1653-1710** *(BRS 87).* Computerised index **1711-1857.**

There were Peculiars centred around Faringdon, Wantage, West Ilsley, Blewbury, Hungerford and Wokingham, whose records are now split between three record offices.

Those for the **Peculiar of Faringdon** (Great Faringdon and Little Coxwell), **1547-1854,** are also now at the *Berkshire Record Office.* Indexed. Those for Langford (partly Oxon) are at

> **Oxfordshire Archives,** Oxford.

Records of both peculiars are jointly indexed (in MS) with Oxfordshire and Buckinghamshire peculiars, in one series, **1547-1853** (microfilm copy at *Berkshire R.O.,* TS at *Society of Genealogists).* There also is a TS index to Faringdon wills, 1547-1799, wills and bonds, 1800-1854, compiled by the late J.W. Brooks, at the *Society of Genealogists.* Records for **Wantage, 1582-1668,** are also at *Oxon. Archives* and included in this index; later records are at *Wiltshire Record Office.*

> **Wiltshire Record Office,** Trowbridge,

holds probate records for the **Consistory Court of Salisbury, 1526-1857.** Some Berkshire testators are to be found in this court, which had superior jurisdiction to the archdeaconry court of Berkshire. There is a MS index compiled in the 19th century, but this is being superseded by a very wide-ranging card index being compiled at *Wiltshire R.O.*

Records of two **peculiars** including Berkshire parishes are at the *Wiltshire Record Office:*

Wantage (Dean and Canons of Windsor in) Hungerford, West Ilsley, Shalbourne and Wantage). MS and card index to all records from **1669** only to **1840.** For records of Wantage and its hamlets (only) **1582-1668,** see *Oxfordshire Archives.*

Dean of Salisbury (Arborfield, Blewbury with Aston Upthorne, Hurst, Ruscombe, Sandhurst, Sonning and Wokingham; also occasionally places in peculiars of Faringdon and Wantage). MS and card index to all records **1538-1857.** See also a TS index to **Miscellaneous Wills 1555-1730** of which many relate to this court.

There is a tiny collection of wills **1396-1736** for the **Court of the Dean of Windsor,** at

> **The Aerary, St. George's Chapel,** Dean's Cloister, Windsor Castle, Berks.

These relate only to a few inhabitants of the castle.

Berkshire FHS have an index to **Berkshire wills beneficiaries** (mainly for Wantage): details from *Tom & Rita Hine, Oakley Cottage, Westbury Lane, Purley on Thames RG8 8DL.*

Berkshire parishes outside the jurisdiction of the archdeacon of Berkshire.

Peculiars: F - Faringdon; **S** - Dean of Salisbury; **W**- Dean and Canons of Windsor in Wantage.

Arborfield **S6**; Aston Upthorne **S3**; Blewbury **S3**; Little Coxwell **F1**; Great Faringdon **F1**; Hungerford **W5**; Hurst **S6**; West Ilsley **W4**; Ruscombe **S6**; Shalbourne (part Wilts.) **W5**; Sonning **S6**; Upton **S3**; Wantage **W2**; Wokingham **S6**.

BERKSHIRE

Wilts.

Oxon.

Bucks.

Archdeaconry of Berkshire

Archdeaconry of Berkshire

Hants.

Surrey

BUCKINGHAMSHIRE
(southern tip now in Berkshire)

Since 1858: Probate records for England and Wales are at the *Principal Registry of the Family Division, Somerset House, Strand London WC2R 1LP*. Indexes to these (to 1928) are held locally at the *Bodleian Library, Oxford*; and on microfiche at the *Centre for Oxfordshire Studies, Oxford Central Library*. See also page 11.

Before 1858: Buckinghamshire formed the archdeaconry of Buckingham in the diocese of Lincoln and province of Canterbury.

For **P.C.C.** (see also page 12), there is an index to Bucks. wills and admons., **1700-1800**, published by Bucks. F.H.S., 1993; and see right. Otherwise most probate records for the county are at

> **Buckinghamshire Record Office, Aylesbury**

and are described in a leaflet *Notes for the Guidance of Genealogists*. The **Archdeaconry of Buckingham** covered virtually the whole county apart from peculiars. There is an index to all probate records, wills **1483-1857**, admons **1632-1857**, for publication by *BRS* and *Bucks. Record Society* in 1995.

The Courts of the Archdeaconry of Buckingham 1483-1523 (*Bucks. Record Society* **19**, 1975) includes many wills.

Records of most **Peculiars**, formerly at Oxford, are now also at the *Bucks. R.O.* These included Aylesbury and Buckingham, and other places listed right. All probate records are indexed jointly with Oxfordshire and Berkshire peculiars in a good 19th cent. index (MS at *Oxon. Archives*, microfilm at *Bucks. R.O.*), in theory from 1547 but in fact most start much later (Aylesbury 1624, Buckingham few pre-1701).

Records of the **Peculiar of Bierton** (incl. also Buckland, Stoke Mandeville and Quarrendon), indexed as above, mostly are at

> **Oxfordshire Archives, Oxford,**

though register copy wills **1701-1708** and **1851-1857** are now at the *Bucks. R.O.*

The present or former Bucks parishes of Caversfield, Ipstone, Lillingstone Lovell and Stokenchurch were in the diocese and archdeaconry of **Oxford**, records at *Oxon. Archives*, see page 43.

Hertfordshire Record Office has records of Aston Abbots, Granborough, Little Horwood and Winslow, in the **Archdeaconry of St. Albans** (see page 30). An index is held by the Bucks F.H.S. for eventual publication. These places may also be found in the **Consistory Court of London** (page 36).

The only other probate records for Buckinghamshire are a small collection, Eton parishioners only, **1457-1666**, kept at **'Penzance', Eton College,** *Berks.*

Published: *Buckinghamshire Probate Inventories, 1661-1714 (Bucks. R.S .24)*, has transcripts for 159 inventories from P.C.C. [PROB.4 and 5].

Buckinghamshire parishes outside the jurisdiction of the archdeacon of Buckingham:

A: Archdeaconry of St. Albans
B: Peculiar of Bierton *(Bodleian)*
O: Diocese and Archdeaconry of Oxford
P: Other Peculiars *(Bucks. R.O.)*

Aston Abbots **A4**; Aylesbury **P6**; Bierton **B7**; Buckingham **P2**; Buckland **B9**; Caversfield (det.) **O**; Eton **14**; Granborough **A3**; Halton **P10**; Little Horwood **A3**; Ibstone or Ipstone **0-13**; Lillingstone Lovell **0-1**; Monks Risborough **P12**; Quarrendon **B5**; Stoke Mandeville **B8**; Stokenchurch **0-13**; Towersey **P11**; Winslow **A3**.

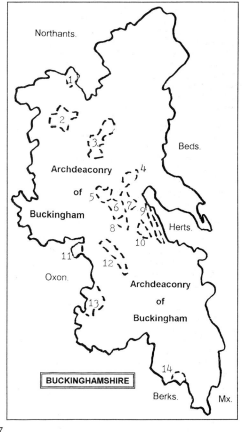

CAMBRIDGESHIRE and the ISLE of ELY

See *Genealogical Sources in Cambridgeshire* by Michael Farrar, Cambs. R.O., 2nd edition, 1994.

Since 1858: Probate records for England and Wales are at the *Principal Registry of the Family Division, Somerset House, Strand London WC2R 1LP.* Indexes to these (to 1966) are held locally at the *County Record Office (Cambridgeshire C.C.), Cambridge;* for other copies, see page 11.

Registered copy wills proved at Peterborough, 1858-1941 (Cambridgeshire, Huntingdonshire and northern Northamptonshire to 1926) are deposited at *Northamptonshire Record Office, Northampton,* and are indexed.

Before 1858: Cambridgeshire was in the province of Canterbury and diocese of Ely.

Apart from P.C.C. (see page 12), most probate records for the county are held at the

---
Cambridgeshire Record Office, *Cambridge.*

Of the two main collections of probate records, much the larger is that of the **Consistory Court of Ely** (and Cambridge). This covered most of the county, with the exceptions noted below.

Index: Wills **1449-1857**, admons **1562-1857**, invs, published by *BRS* in 3 parts. *(BRS 103, 106, 107).*

The other main collection is that of the **Archdeaconry of Ely** which included Cambridge itself, and parishes in the south-west of the county. Note that records for these places may also be found in the Consistory Court, above.

Published index: **1513-1857** (all records) *(BRS 88).*

There are also two small collections:

Peculiar of Thorney: **1774-1857** (calendar to all records);

Peculiar of the Dean and Chapter of Ely: confined to Ely Cathedral Close **1565-1800** (to be included in *BRS* Consistory Court index volumes).

Cambridge University Library

(for which prior application for a reader's ticket must be made to *The Keeper of the University Archives, The University Library, Cambridge*)
---

holds the records of the **Court of the Chancellor (or Vice-Chancellor) of the University of Cambridge.** This was confined to members of the university and others connected with it, including some Cambridge townspeople

Another small collection is at *King's College, Cambridge*, for the **Peculiar of King's College, Cambridge, 1449-1794,** confined to the precincts of King's College.

Probate records for parishes around Newmarket on the east of the county in the **Archdeaconry of Sudbury** are at the *Suffolk Record Office, Bury St. Edmunds.* Modern indexes, **1439-1857** (published to 1700, *BRS 95, 96*), to all records, see page 39.

Archdeaconry of Ely ('**7**' on map unless otherwise stated):

Cambridge (all parishes) **6**; Abington Pigotts; Bassingbourn; Bourn; Boxworth; Caldecote; Caxton; Cherry Hinton **6**; Conington; Croxton; Croydon cum Clopton; Elsworth; Eltisley; Gt and Lit Eversden; Fen Drayton; Fulbourn **6**; Gamlingay; Guilden Morden; Graveley; Haddenham **6**; East Hatley; Hatley St. George; Kingston; Knapwell; Litlington; Lolworth; Longstowe; Melbourn; Meldreth; Papworth St. Agnes and Everard; Shingay; Steeple Morden; Swavesey; Tadlow; Toft; Wendy with Shingay; Whaddon; Wilburton **5**.

Parishes outside the jurisdiction of the Consistory Court of Ely:

Archdeaconry of Sudbury, 4
Ashley cum Silverley; Burwell; Cheveley; Chippenham; Wood Ditton; Fordham; Kennett; Kirtling; Landwade; Newmarket All Saints; Snailwell; Soham; Wicken.

Archdeaconry of Norfolk, 2
Outwell, Upwell, Welney.

Peculiars of Isleham, 3, and **Thorney, 1.**

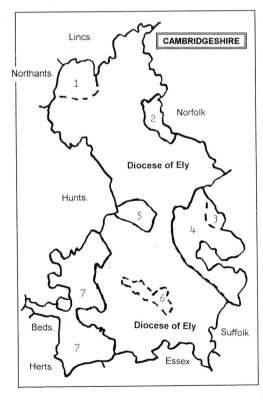

Cambridgeshire, continued

Also at the *Suffolk Record Office, Bury St. Edmunds*, are records of the **Peculiar of Isleham** (Cambs.) **and Freckenham** (Suffolk), for which there is a card index, **1556-1581, 1613-1636, 1647-1857** (admons, invs from 1662 only), pre-1701 entries also in BRS *95, 96.*

Records for these parishes may also be found in the consistory courts of Norwich (page 38), Rochester (page 32) and (after 1649) the archdeaconry court of Huntingdon (page 31).

Records of three parishes in the north-east of the county, Outwell, Upwell, and Welney, in the **Archdeaconry of Norfolk**, are at *Norfolk Record Office*. There are published indexes to wills 1453-1602; see page 38 for these and other indexes.

CHESHIRE

(northern border now in Greater Manchester; Wirral in Merseyside)

Since 1858: Probate records for England and Wales are at the *Principal Registry of the Family Division, Somerset House, Strand, London WC2R 1LP.* Indexes to these are held locally by *Cheshire R.O.* (to 1929) and *Greater Manchester R.O.* For further copies, see page 11.

Registered copy wills proved at Chester, 1858-1940 (Cheshire only to 1926), are deposited at *Cheshire R.O.* and are indexed.

Before 1858: Cheshire was in the diocese of Chester and province of York - for P.C.Y., see page 56; for P.C.C., see page 12.

Apart from P.C.Y. and P.C.C. all probate records for the county are held at

Cheshire Record Office, *Chester.*

The **Consistory Court of Chester** covered the entire county from the creation of the diocese in 1541. There are no peculiars in the county.

Indexes have been published by the *Lancs. & Ches. Record Soc.* to wills and admons, **1545-1837,** with the prospect of further volumes to come. For the period **1751-1837** these have been superseded by 6 volume index published by Cheshire Record Office.

Meanwhile there is a TS index to the remaining years, **1838-1857.**

In this diocese only, estates worth less than £40 were kept in a separate 'infra' series, and in the published index volumes are in a separate volume before 1665, and in appendices from 1660 to 1800. Since 1800 they have been indexed jointly with the main series. To 1820 Cheshire and Lancashire wills and admons are intermingled in the indexes, but from 1821 they are in separate sections in each volume.

Lancs. & Ches. Record Soc. vols.:
1545-1650 (main series), *2* and *4;*
1590-1665 (infra series), *52;*
1660-1800, *15, 18, 20, 22, 25, 37, 38, 44, 45;*
1801-1820, *62, 63, 78*
1821-1837 (Cheshire separate) *107, 113, 118, 120.*

Vols. *33, 43, 52* list miscellaneous wills **1487-1800;** and additional wills and admons for **1670** and **1693** are in vol. *63.*

See also *Stockport Probate Records, 1578-1619, 1620-1650,* ed. C.B. Phillips and J.H. Smith, *Lancs & Ches RS, 124, 131* (1985, 1992) (full transcripts of 118 wills and inventories), and *Stockport in the Mid-Seventeenth Century (1660-1669),* ed. S. McKenna and C.M. Nunn, *Stockport Hist. Soc.,* 1992 (analysis of 44 wills and inventories).

For a map of the county, see page 56.

CORNWALL

Since 1858: Probate records for England and Wales are at the *Principal Registry of the Family Division, Somerset House, Strand London WC2R 1LP.* Indexes to these are held locally by the *Probate Sub-registry, Market Street, Bodmin.* For other copies, see page 11.

Registered copy wills proved at Bodmin, 1858-1941 (only Cornwall to 1926) are deposited at the *Cornwall Record Office,* and are indexed by parish to 1929. Original wills, 1858-1969, are still at *Bodmin Probate Sub-Registry.*

Before 1858: Cornwall formed the archdeaconry of Cornwall in the diocese of Exeter and province of Canterbury.

Apart from P.C.C. (see page 12), most probate records for the county are at

> **Cornwall Record Office,** *Truro*
> (appointment essential).

See *Guide to Cornish Probate Records,* Cornwall R.O.

These mainly comprise the **Consistory Court of the Archdeaconry of Cornwall,** printed index to wills and admons **1600-1799** (and a very few pre-1600) *(BRS 56, 59)*; these also include the tiny **Royal Peculiar of St. Buryan 1600-1799** (in a separate section). This published index has been superseded at the *Cornwall R.O.* by a card index with fuller and additional information, itself for eventual complete publication: **1600-1649** (five parts, A-D, E-K, L-R, S-Z, parishes and occupations, pub. 1985-8), £2.00 each part + 50p p&p. There is a separate MS index to St. Buryan records.

For **1800-1857** there is a consolidated TS index, which also includes Estate Duty Office wills and admons for courts whose records have been destroyed (see below), 1812-1857. This index has been published on microfiche by *BRS (M'fiche 1).*

Records of the **Episcopal Consistory Court of Exeter** and **Episcopal Principal Registry of Exeter** were destroyed by enemy action in 1942. These courts had some jurisdiction throughout the county (particularly over clergy) and included all records for 22 Cornish parishes in peculiars (listed right). The lost records are indexed in *BRS **35*** (Principal Registry) **1559-1799,** and *BRS **46*** (Consistory) **1532-1800.**

Records of the **Peculiars of the Dean and Chapter of Exeter,** which included five Cornish parishes (see opposite) were also destroyed. See Glencross's calendar at *Soc. of Gen.,* right.

Post-1811 Death Duty Office copies of wills and admons from these courts are now at the *Cornwall Record Office.* Abstracts of wills and admons, **1796-1811,** for these and other courts should still be found in Death Duty Registers at the *Public Record Office,* page 14. The *Devon and Cornwall Record Society* has a microfilm of the index to these.

The *Society of Genealogists* has a TS calendar to Cornish wills and admons (mainly pre-1814, ?incomplete) in P.C.C. and Exeter courts, compiled before 1942 by J.R.M. Glencross.

Parishes in peculiars:
B = Bishop of Exeter; **D** = Dean and Chapter of Exeter; **S** = St. Buryan.

St. Agnes **D5**; St. Anthony in Roseland **B7**; Boconnock with Bradoc **D3**; St. Breoke **B2**; Budock **B6**; (St.) Buryan **S8**; Egloshayle **B2**; St. Erney **B4**; St. Ervan **B2**; St. Eval **B2**; Falmouth **B6**; (St.) Germans **B4**; (St.) Gerrans **B7**; St. Gluvias **B6**; St. Issey **B2**; Landrake **B1**; Lawhitton **B1**; St. Levan **S8**; Lezant **B1**; Mabe **B6**; St. Merryn **B2**; Mylor **B6**; Padstow **B2**; Perranzabulo **D5**; Little Petherick (or St. Petroc Minor) **B2**; South Petherwyn **B1**; Sennen **S8**; Trewen **B1**; St. Winnow **D3**.

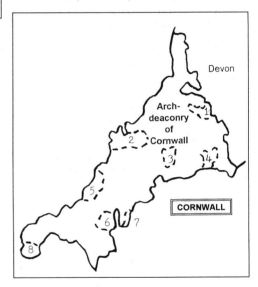

CUMBERLAND and WESTMORLAND
(now both in Cumbria)

Since 1858: Probate records for England and Wales are at the *Principal Probate Registry of the Family Division, Somerset House, Strand, London WC2R 1LP.* Indexes to these (to 1928) are held locally at the *Cumbria Record Office, Carlisle.*

Registered copy wills proved at Carlisle (only Cumberland and Westmorland to 1926) are deposited at the *Cumbria Record Office, Carlisle,* and are indexed to 1941.

Cumberland and Westmorland, continued

Before 1858: Cumberland and Westmorland were in the diocese of Carlisle and Chester and in the province of York. For records of P.C.Y., see page 56, and also records of P.C.C., page 12.

Apart from P.C.Y. and P.C.C., the probate records for these two counties are split between Carlisle and Preston.

Cumbria Record Office, Carlisle

holds records of the **Consistory Court of Carlisle,** which had jurisdiction over the major part of Cumberland and the northern half of Westmorland. See *Cumbrian Ancestors* (Cumbria Archive Service, 2nd edition, 1993, £4.99).

Records (wills and admons) start in **1564,** with a C19 MS index which is being superseded: **1600-1616,** work in progress; **1617-1644,** card index; **1661-1750,** TS index, for publication by *BRS*; **1751-1857,** card index; also 1858-1941 (see left). Microfilms of wills and of the original MS index, and the 1661-1750 TS, are at *Cumbria Record Office, Kendal.*

There were three manorial courts in Westmorland (but within the diocese of Carlisle), records at *Cumbria R.O. Carlisle* (separately card indexed), with microfilms at *Cumbria R.O., Kendal:*

Ravenstonedale, 1691-1857;
Temple Sowerby, 1580-1816;
Docker, 1696-1770 (a few only).

Lancashire Record Office, Preston

holds the records of the **Consistory Court of the Commissary of the Archdeaconry of Richmond (Western Deaneries),** which had jurisdiction over the remainder of the two counties, the south-west of Cumberland (deanery of Copeland) and the southern part of Westmorland (deaneries of Kendal and Lonsdale, both partly in Lancashire). Microfilms of Deanery of Copeland wills are at the *C.R.O, Carlisle* and *Kendal* (1748-1798). *C.R.O. Kendal* also has microfilm of Kendal Deanery, 1538-1860.

There is a 19th cent. MS index to wills and admons, **1457-1720,** and a calendar to the remainder, **1720-1857.** Lists of Cumberland (deanery of Copeland) wills **1530-1726,** (and Copeland Act Book, 1727-48, index 1727-51) are also at the *Cumbria Record Office* branches at *Carlisle, Kendal* and *Barrow* (with a modern listing in progress). The indexes to the western deaneries printed by the *Lancs. and Cheshire Record Society* do not include non-Lancashire wills.

Exceptions:
Alston and Garrigill, and (until 1703) Upper or Over Denton, all in Cumberland, were in the jurisdiction of the Consistory Court of Durham, see page 25.

Parishes outside the jurisdiction of the consistory court of Carlisle:

Archdeaconry of Richmond, diocese of Chester:

Cumberland (Deanery of Copeland), 4
Arlecdon, Beckermet St. Bridget and St. John, Bootle, Brigham, Buttermere, Cleator, Clifton, Cockermouth, Corney, Dean, Distington, Drigg, Egremont, Embleton, Ennerdale, Eskdale, Gosforth, Harrington, Hensingham, Irton, Lamplugh, Lorton, Loweswater, Millom, Moresby, Mosser, Muncaster, Ponsonby, St. Bees, Setmurthy, Thwaites, Ulpha, Waberthwaite, Wasdalehead, Nether Wasdale, Whicham, Whitbeck, Whitehaven, Workington, Wythop.

Westmorland (deaneries of Kendal and Lonsdale), 5
Ambleside, Barbon, Beetham, Burnside, Burton in Kendal, Casterton, Crook, Crosthwaite, Firbank, Grasmere, Greyrigg, Holme, New and Old Hutton, Hutton Roof, Hugill (Ings), Kendal, Kentmere, Killington, Kirby Lonsdale, Langdale, Mansergh, Middleton, Preston Patrick, Rydal, Selside, Long Sleddale, Over Staveley, Troutbeck, Underbarrow, Windermere, Winster, Witherslack.

Diocese of Durham, Alston with Garrigill, Cumb., **2:** Upper Denton, Cumb., **1.**

Peculiar of Ravenstonedale, 6
Peculiar of Temple Sowerby, 3.

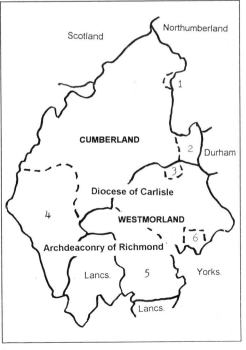

21

DERBYSHIRE
see with **Staffordshire**, pages 46-48.

DEVON

Since 1858: Probate records for England and Wales are at the *Principal Registry of the Family Division, Somerset House, Strand, London WC2R 1LP*. Indexes to these are held locally at the *Probate Sub-Registry, Eastgate House, High Street, Exeter EX4 3JU*. For other copies, see page 11.

Before 1858: Devon was in the province of Canterbury and diocese of Exeter.

Apart from P.C.C. (see page 12), all probate records for the county and the diocese of Exeter (except Cornwall) were destroyed by enemy action in 1942.

Prior to this calamity, indexes to wills and admons in three important courts had been published. These were:

Episcopal Consistory Court of Exeter, 1532-1800 *(BRS 46)*, jurisdiction throughout the county.

Episcopal Principal Registry of Exeter, 1599-1799 *(BRS 35)*, jurisdiction throughout the county and sole jurisdiction in 14 Devon parishes which were peculiars of the bishop.

Consistory Court of the Archdeaconry of Exeter, 1547-1799 *(BRS 35)*, jurisdiction in that archdeaconry.

Devon, continued

Copies of a TS index to the lost wills and admons of the **Consistory Court of the Archdeaconry of Barnstaple, 1563-1857**, are at the *Westcountry Studies Library (Exeter Central Library), Exeter University*, the *North Devon Athenaeum* at *Barnstaple*, and *New York Public Library*.

No index survives to the lost records of the **Archdeaconry of Totnes**.

Devon Record Office, *Exeter*

(Family History leaflet available) has a large and partially indexed collection of copies of wills from numerous sources, particularly those made by Miss Moger. It also has Estate Duty Office copy wills from all Devon courts, 1812-1857. The *Westcountry Studies Library* has collections by Miss Moger and Oswyn Murray.

Wills and Admons 1796-1811 should be found in the Death Duty Registers at the *Public Record Office*, see page 14. The *Devon and Cornwall Record Society* has a microfilm of the index to these Estate Duty Office abstracts.

There are also copies of wills at the *West Devon Record Office, Plymouth*.

Records for a few places not deposited at the destroyed Exeter Probate Registry include:

Cornwall Record Office, *Truro:*

North Petherwin, St. Giles in the Heath and Werrington, in the **Consistory Court of the Archdeaconry of Cornwall**, page 20.

Dorset Record Office, *Dorchester:*

Stockwood and Dalwood (detached Dorset parishes) in **Consistory Court of Bristol (Dorset Division)** and **Archdeaconry of Dorset**, see page 23.

Wiltshire Record Office, *Trowbridge*

Uffculme, in the **Prebend of Uffculme, 1552-1857** (MS Index); see also page 53.

Key to jurisdictions of places listed on page 23.

AC : Archdeaconry of Cornwall;
AD : Archdeaconry of Dorset;
AE : Archdeaconry of Exeter (outlying parishes);
BE : Bishop of Exeter's Peculiars;
C : Manor of Cockington;
DC : Dean and Chapter of Exeter's Peculiars;
DE : Dean of Exeter's Peculiar;
T : Manor of Templeton;
U : Prebend of Uffculme;
VC : Peculiar of Vicars Choral

Devon, continued

Parishes in Devon outside the jurisdiction of the archdeaconries of Barnstaple, Exeter and Totnes. For key, see left.

Ashburton **DC27**; Bickington **DC27**; Bishops Nympton **BE5**; Bishops Tawton **BE4**; Bishops Teignton **BE26**; Branscombe **DC21**; Braunton **DE2**; Buckland-in-the-Moor **DC27**; Chudleigh **BE24**; Clyst Honiton **DC20**; Cockington **C30**; Coffinswell **DC29**; Colebrook **DC12**; Colyton **DC16**; Combeinteignhead **AE28**; Crediton **BE11**; Culmstock **DC8**; Dalwood **AD&AE14**; Dawlish **DC25**; Down St. Mary **AE10**; Exeter Cathedral Close **DE**; Exmouth **DC23**; Heavitree **DC19**; Ide **DC18**; Kennerleigh **BE11**; Kingskerswell **DC29**; Landkey **BE4**; Littleham (nr. Exmouth) **DC23**; Marldon **BE29**; Monkton **DC13**; Morchard Bishop **BE11**; Northcott **AC17**; E & W Ogwell **AE28**; Paignton **BE30**; N Petherwin **AC17**; St. Giles in the Heath **AC17**; St. Marychurch **DC29**; Salcombe Regis **DC21**; Sandford **BE11**; Shaldon **AE28**; Shute **DC16**; Sidbury **DC21**; Staverton **DC27**; Stockland **AD&AE14**; Stoke Canon **DC19**; Stoke Gabriel **BE30**; Stokeinteignhead **AE28**; Swimbridge **BE4**; East Teignmouth **DC25**; West Teignmouth **BE26**; Templeton **T6**; Thorncombe **AE&AD15**; Topsham **DC19**; Uffculme **U9**; Werrington **AC17**; Woodbury **VC22**.

DORSET

Since 1858: Probate records for England and Wales are at the *Principal Registry of the Family Division, Somerset House, Strand, London WC2R 1LP.* Indexes to these are held locally at the *Bristol R.O.* (to 1900); *Exeter Sub-Registry* (see page 11); and the *Hampshire R.O., Winchester* (to 1932); for other copies see page 11.

Registered copy wills proved at Blandford, 1858-1941, are deposited at the *Dorset R.O.* and are indexed.

Before 1858: Dorset formed the archdeaconry of Dorset in the diocese of Bristol and province of Canterbury.

Indexes to **P.C.C.** wills for Dorset, **1383-1700** (printed) and **1701-1820** (MS); and admons **1559-1725** (printed, *Somerset & Dorset Notes & Queries, vols.* **2-6**) and **1726-1821** (MS), all included in card index at *Dorset Record Office;* copy of these indexes at *SofG.* See page 12.

Index to **P.C.C.** *Wills* **1821-58**, compiled by Miriam Scott, Arthur Golding and Margaret Spearman, published by *Somerset & Dorset F.H.S.*, 1992.

Apart from P.C.C., most probate records for Dorset are held at the

---
Dorset Record Office, *Dorchester.*

There is a consolidated card index to *all* these, including *all* local courts as well as P.C.C. before 1858, and the later Dorset Probate Registry records. This supersedes the various printed indexes (usually to all records).

The main courts for the county were the **Archdeaconry Court of Dorset** (index **1660-1792**, *BRS 22*, pp 25-179) and the much smaller **Consistory Court of Bristol (Dorset Division)**, which only had occasional jurisdiction (index **1681-1792**, *BRS 22*, pp. 1-24). A few records of these two courts will also be found in *BRS 53* (pp. 131-70). All card indexed to 1857.

There are also published lists or indexes, in *BRS 22*, to various Peculiars whose records are at the Dorset Record Office:

Great Canford and Poole, 1639-1799
Corfe Castle, 1577-1799
Milton Abbas, 1675-1811
Sturminster Marshall, 1641-1799
Wimborne Minster, 1590-1823 (also invs **1587-1719**, in *BRS 53*, pp. 129, described mistakenly as belonging to Great Canford and Poole).

There were numerous other peculiar courts in Dorset whose records are now at the *Wiltshire Record Office*. These are all included in the card index at *Dorset Record Office*, although the records themselves are at Trowbridge. Microfilm of these records, excluding the Dean of Salisbury and the Dean and Chapter peculiars, are available at the *Dorset Record Office.*

Indexes to 1799 to all of these were published in *BRS 53*. The courts, with earliest dates for records (wills, admons and invs) are:

Peculiar of the Dean of Salisbury (this had jurisdiction over 28 Dorset parishes), from **1600**;
Peculiar of the Dean and Chapter of Salisbury (included Stourpaine and Durweston in Dorset), **1604-1799**;
Chardstock, 1639-1799;
Fordington and Writhlington, 1660-1799;
Gillingham, 1658-1799;
Lyme Regis and Halstock, 1664-1799;
Netherbury in ecclesia, 1608-1799;
Preston and Sutton Pointz, 1761-1799;
Yetminster and Grimston, 1654-1799.

The *Wiltshire Record Office* has card or MS indexes to records of these courts to 1857.

Dorset, continued

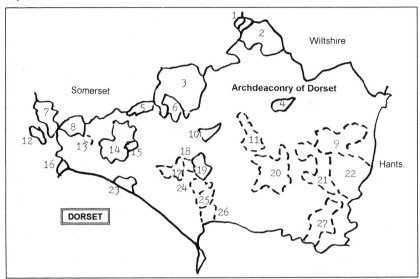

Parishes in Dorset in jurisdictions other than the archdeaconry of Dorset:

Note: records of the prebends of Chardstock, Lyme Regis and Halstock, Netherbury in ecclesia, Preston and Sutton Poyntz, and Yetminster and Grimston are to be found also in the peculiar court of the dean of Salisbury (in addition to the parishes in the direct jurisdiction of that court). Places in the liberty of Frampton also appear in the archdeaconry and consistory records.

BB : Burton Bradstock; **C :** Chardstock; **CC :** Corfe Castle; **CP :** Gt. Canford and Poole; **DC :** Dean and Chapter of Salisbury; **DS :** Dean of Salisbury; **E :** Diocese of Exeter; **F :** Frampton; **FW :** Fordington and Writhlington; **G :** Gillingham; **LR :** Lyme Regis and Halstock; **MA :** Milton Abbas; **N :** Netherbury; **P:** Preston and Sutton Poyntz; **SM :** Sturminster Marshall; **ST :** Stratton; **WM :** Wimborne Minster; **Y :** Yetminster and Grimston.

Alton Pancras **DS10**; Anderson **DS20**; Beaminster **N&DS14**; Bere Hacket **DS3**; Bere Regis **DS20**; Bettiscombe **F13**; Bincombe **F25**; Bloxworth **DS20**; Bourton **G1**; Burton Bradstock **BB23**; Gt Canford **CP22**; Castleton **DS3**; Caundle Marsh **DS3**; Chardstock **C&DS7**; Charminster **DS19**; Chetnole **Y&DS6**; Clifton Maybank **DS3**; Nether Compton **DS3**; Over Compton **DS3**; Compton Valence **F17**; Corfe Castle **CC27**; Corfe Mullen **SM21**; Dalwood (archd. of Dorset, detd.) **12**; Folke **DS3**; Fordington **FW24**; Frampton **F17**; Gillingham **G2**; Grimston **Y18**, Halstock **LR&DS5**; Hamworthy **SM21**; Haydon **DS3**; Hermitage **DS3**; Holnest **DS3**; Kingston **CC27**;

Leigh **Y&DS6**; Lillington **DS3**; Longburton **DS3**; Lyme Regis **LR&DS16**; Lytchett Minster **SM21**; Mapperton **DS15**; Milborne Stileham **DS20**; Milton Abbas **MA11**; Motcombe **G2**; Netherbury **N&DS14**; Oborne **DS3**; Poole **CP22**; Preston **P26**; Ryme Intrinsica **DS3**; Sherborne **DS3**; Stockland (archd. of Dorset, detd.) **12**; Stockwood **DS3**; Stourpaine **DC4**; Stratton **ST&DS18**; Sturminster Marshall **SM21**; Sutton Poyntz **P&DS26**; Thorncombe **E8**; Thornford **DS3**; Tomson **DS20**; Turners Puddle **DS20**; Wambrook **C&DS7**; Wimborne Minster **WM9**; Winterborne Came **F25**; Winterborne Herringstone **F25**; Winterborne Kingston **DS20**; Winterborne Tomson **DS20**; Woolland **MA11**; North Wootton **DS3**; Yetminster **Y&DS6**.

DURHAM and NORTHUMBERLAND
(border area between counties incl. Newcastle now in Tyne and Wear; south-east border of co. Durham now in Cleveland).

Since 1858: Probate records for England and Wales are at the *Principal Registry of the Family Division, Somerset House, Strand, London WC2R 1LP.* For printed copies of indexes elsewhere, see page 11.

Durham and Northumberland, continued

Registered copy wills proved at Newcastle, 1858-1939 (from 1926 also. incl. Gateshead and places immediately south of the River Tyne) are deposited at the *Northumberland Record Office;* those proved at Durham, 1858-1940 (for co. Durham) are deposited at *Durham University Library, Archives and Special Collections.* Originals 1858-1969 are at York Sub-Registry (see page 11).

Before 1858: County Durham and most of Northumberland were in the diocese of Durham in the province of York. For records of P.C.Y., see page 56; and see also records of P.C.C., page 12. Index of Co. Durham and Northumberland wills 1651-1660 (proved P.C.C.), TS, at the *Society of Genealogists.*

Apart from P.C.Y. and P.C.C., nearly all probate records for both counties are housed by the

Durham University Library Archives and Special Collections, Durham

(no special reader's ticket required, but searchers are required to register and produce proof of identity and of their permanent address).

The **Consistory Court of Durham** covered all of both counties (except for a peculiar, below). There are card indexes to wills, admons, invs **1540-1681** (superseding the printed index 1540-99 *(Newcastle upon Tyne Records Committee Publication 8)* and the TS index 1540-1812 by J.W. Robinson, at *SofG* and *Newcastle upon Tyne Ref. Library*) and 1832-1857. The intervening period 1682-1831 is covered by older MS calendars. Work on extending the replacement card index beyong 1681 is on-going. M'f copies of older MS calendars at *Cleveland Archives Dept., Middlesbrough, Durham County Record Office* and *Newcastle upon Tyne Central Library.*

The only other probate records for the counties are at the

Borthwick Institute , York (see page 56).

Peculiar of the Archbishop of York in Hexham and Hexhamshire (until 1837 only):
Hexham with Whitley; Allendale with West Allen, St Peter's Allenheads and Ninebanks; St. John Lee with St. Oswald's and St. Mary Bingfield; all in N'humbd. Printed index: probate act book, **1593-1602** (260 only) (*Yorks. Arch. Soc. R.S. 60*, pp. 184-189). After 1600 records of the court are merged with P.C.Y., p. 46; also some wills and invs, **1694-1706**, at *Northumberland R.O.,* index in *J. N'hmbd & Durham FHS 6* 2 (Jan 81); and the **Peculiar of the Prebend of Tockerington** (jurisdiction: Throckrington in Northumberland). A few records, **1741-1744.**

Printed:
Personal Names in Wills Proved at Durham 1787-1791, G. Nicholson & J.A. Readdie, N&D FHS, 1994.
Darlington Wills and Inventories 1600-1625, (*Surtees Society vol. 201*, 1993).
See also *Surtees Soc. vols. 2, 38, 112, 142.*

ESSEX
(partly now in Greater London)

Since 1858: Probate records for England and Wales are at the *Principal Registry of the Family Division, Somerset House, Strand, London WC2R 1LP.* For printed copies of indexes elsewhere see page 11.

Registered copy wills proved at Ipswich, 1858-1941 (for north Essex only, to 1926) are deposited locally at the *Ipswich* branch of the *Suffolk Record Office,* and are indexed.

Before 1858: Essex was in the province of Canterbury and diocese of London. For P.C.C., see page 12. Abstracts of all Essex wills in P.C.C. 1558-1603 (339) are published in *Elizabethan Life* vol. **4**. *Wills of Essex Gentry and Merchants.* Apart from P.C.C. most of the probate records for the county are held at

Essex Record Office, Chelmsford.

There is a published index to all wills at the Office, for all courts in one sequence, **1400-1619, 1620-1720, 1721-1857** *(BRS 78, 79, 84),* which covers almost the whole county. These comprise the **Archdeaconries of Colchester** (from 1500), **Essex** (from 1400) and **Middlesex** (Essex & Herts div; from 1554). and **Bishop of London's Commissary** (Essex and Herts div; from 1483) as well as the **Peculiars of Writtle with Roxwell** (from 1607) **Good Easter** (from 1613), **Bocking** (post-1620) and the **Sokens** (post-1620); in *BRS* **79** these are listed out of place, pages vii-viii).

Abstracts of 278 wills from these courts, **1558-1603** are published in *Elizabethan Life*, vol. **5**: *Wills of Essex Gentry and Yeomen;* abstracts of *all* the remainder of the three Archdeaconry Courts are published in *Essex Wills,* vol. **1, 1558-1565** (1,002), vol. **2, 1565-1571** (880), vol. **3, 1571-1577** (1,050), vol. **4 1577-1584** (1,004); vol. **5, 1583-1592** (1,299), vol. **6, 1591-1597** (1,135), vol. **7, 1597-1603** (971), and Commissary Court, **1558-1603,** vol. **8, 1558-1569,** vol. **9,** 1569-1578; vols. **10-12,** in preparation.

Admons are calendared separately (MS only) and commence: **Commissary Court of London 1619; Archdeaconries of Colchester 1663; Essex 1559; Middlesex 1660; Peculiars of Bocking 1665; Good Easter 1613; Sokens 1632; Writtle 1637.**

Invs for the **Peculiar of Writtle** are published in *Farm and Cottage Inventories* by F.W. Steer (**C17-18**, 250).

There is an **Index to Wills Beneficiaries** in wills at *Essex R.O.,* complete for the whole county **1721-1858;** in progress, 1625-1720; details and fees for searches from *Mrs Thora Broughton, 43 Pertwee Drive, Chelmsford CM2 8DY.*

Essex, continued

Some Essex probate records are to be found at

> **London Metropolitan Archives** (formerly Greater London Record Office), London

in the **Consistory Court of London**. At present there are only MS calendars, **1514-1669** (a few earlier) to wills and chronological lists to wills **1669-1857**, admons **1540-1857**; but a full index to wills, **1492-1719**, in preparation for publication by *BRS*.

Exceptions:

> **Guildhall Library,** London

holds records of the **London Division** of the **Commissary Court of London,** which includes places in Essex on the outskirts of London: Chingford, Epping, Leyton, Loughton, Nazeing, Waltham Holy Cross, Walthamstow and Woodford, Published index, wills and admons **1374-1625** (*BRS 82, 86, 97*; **1626-1700** waiting publication). MS calendar only to unpublished period to 1857. Abstracts of Essex wills, **1558-1603** (418) published in *Elizabethan Wills of South-West Essex*.

Guildhall Library, London also holds records of the **Peculiar of the Dean and Chapter of St. Paul's,** which includes places scattered throughout Essex: Barling, Belchamp St. Pauls, Heybridge, Navestock, Tillingham, and Wickham St. Pauls.

Index (MS, 19th cent.) wills **1535-1672**; calendar only, wills **1672-1840**, admons **1646-1837**. Full index in preparation for publication by *BRS*.

Probate records of St. Mary Maldon in the **Royal Peculiar of the Dean and Chapter of Westminster** are at the **City of Westminster Archives Centre,** London. See page 36.

Probate records for the **Peculiar of Hornchurch** are at **New College,** Oxford: wills **1767-1839** (10), admons **1766, 1832, 1836** (calendar at Essex R.O. and SofG).

Parishes in Essex outside the main jurisdiction of the commissary court of London (Essex & Herts div) and the archdeaconries of Colchester, Essex and Middlesex:
L = commissary court of London (London div.);
Peculiars: **B** = Bocking; **GE** = Good Easter;
P = dean and chapter of St.Paul's; **S** = Sokens;
W = Writtle with Roxwell; **Z** = dean and chapter of Westminster (not marked on map).

Barling **P14**; Belchamp St.Pauls **P1**; Bocking **B3**; Borley **B**; Chingford **L11**; Chrishall **Z**; Little Coggeshall **B**; Good Easter **GE5 & Z**; Epping **L11**; Heybridge **P6**; Kirkby-le-Soken **S4**; Latchingdon **B10**; Leyton **L11**; Loughton **L11**; Maldon St. Mary **Z**; Milton in Prittlewell **B15**; Navestock **P12**; Nazeing **L11**; Newport **Z**; Roxwell **W7**; Runsell in Danbury **B8**; Southchurch **B15**; Stisted **B3**; Thorpe-le-Soken **S4**; Tillingham **P9**; Waltham Holy Cross **L11**; Walthamstow **L11**; Walton-le-Soken **S4**; Wickham St. Paul's **P2**; Woodford **L11**; Writtle **W7**.

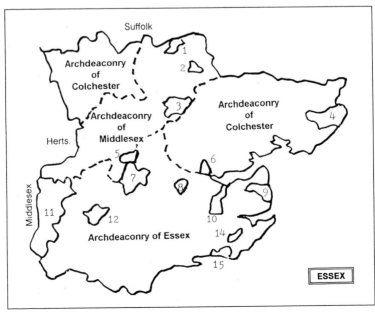

GLOUCESTERSHIRE and BRISTOL

Since 1858: Probate records for England and Wales are at the *Principal Registry of the Family Division, Somerset House, Strand, London WC2R 1LP*. Indexes to these are held locally at the *Gloucestershire Record Office* (to 1936) and the **Bristol Record Office** (to 1900).

Registered copy wills proved at Gloucester, 1858-1941 are deposited at the *Gloucestershire Record Office*, and are indexed to 1941. Registered copy wills proved at Bristol, 1858-1941 (Bristol and Bath County Court districts to 1926) are deposited at the *Bristol Record Office*; index 1858-91. Original wills pre-1926 are now at the *Public Record Office*; later original wills are still at the *Bristol Probate Registry, Ground Floor, The Crescent Centre, Temple Back, Bristol BS1 6EP*.

Before 1858: Gloucestershire and the city of Bristol were in the province of Canterbury. Most of the county was in the diocese of Gloucester, but the city of Bristol, comprising seventeen parishes, and several neighbouring parishes in Gloucestershire, were in the diocese of Bristol; and also four Somerset parishes.

Most probate records for the county, apart from P.C.C. (see page 12) are at

Gloucestershire Record Office, *Gloucester*
(daily charge)

which publishes a full guide in *Gloucestershire Family History*. Apart from the Bristol area virtually the whole county is covered by the **Consistory Court of Gloucester**, for which there are published indexes to wills, **1541-1650** *(BRS 12)* and to wills **1660-1800** and admons **1684-1800** *(BRS 34)*; Wills and admons **1801-58** *(BRS m'fiche 4*, 1996).

Wills proved in Gloucestershire Peculiar Courts indexes probate records (also at the *Glos. R.O.*) for the **Peculiars of Bibury** (incl. Aldsworth, Barnsley and Winson) **1619-1833**; **Bishops Cleeve** (and Stoke Orchard) **1622-1765**; and **Withington** (and Dowdeswell) **1624-1776**. Partial indexes also in *BRS 12*; and see Consistory.

The *Glos. R.O.* has TS indexes to two collections of miscellaneous wills and invs, pre-1858, found at the probate registry, not included in the printed calendars.

Bristol Record Office, *Bristol*

holds probate records for Bristol and neighbouring Gloucestershire parishes (listed right) which were covered by the **Consistory Court of the Bishop of Bristol in the Deanery of Bristol**. There is a printed index to wills **1568-1792** and admons **1770-1793** *(BRS 17)*; MS calendars to wills and admons to **1857**; admons **1661-1769** (index in progress); invs **1609-1767** (indexed).

Published: *Bristol Tudor Wills* (1546-1603) (Calendar/abstracts of 192 city of Bristol wills) (*Bristol Record Society 44*, 1993); *Bristol wills 1546-1593, 1597-1598*, 2 vols. TS reproduction; *Guide to the Probate Inventories of Bristol Deanery 1542-1804* (Bristol Record Society and Bristol & Gloucestershire Archaeoogical Society, 1988); *Clifton and Westbury probate invs, 1609-1761* (Bristol University, 1981).

For Bristol wills see also the Bristol Great Orphan Books (at *Bristol R.O.*), also indexed in BRS 17.

See also the *Guide to the Bristol Archives Office and the Diocese of Bristol: a catalogue of the records of the Bishop and Archdeacons and of the Dean and Chapter* (1970).

Places in the jurisdiction of the **Consistory Court of Bristol**:

All parishes in the city of **Bristol**;
the **Gloucestershire** parishes of: Almondesbury, Alveston, Clifton, Compton Greenfield, Elberton, Filton, Henbury, Horfield, St.George Bristol, Littleton-on-Severn, Mangotsfield, Olveston, Stapleton, Stoke Gifford, Westbury-on-Trym, Winterbourne St.Michael; and Abbots Leigh (Som.); Bedminster (Som.) (from 1845 only).

Peculiars:
Bibury, 3: Aldsworth, Barnsley, Bibury, Winson.
Bishops Cleeve, 1: Bishops Cleeve, Stoke Orchard.
Withington, 2: Dowdeswell, Withington.

Note. Shenington, formerly in Glos., now in Oxon, was in the diocese of Gloucester until 1837 when it was transferred to the diocese of Worcester.

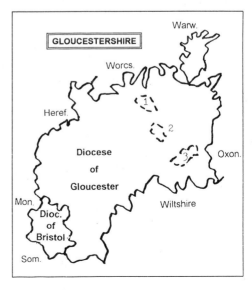

Hampshire parishes and places in peculiars. In area '11' unless otherwise indicated. All were also subject to the consistory court and most are also likely to appear in the archdeaconry court.

Allington; New and Old Alresford; Alverstoke **18**; Ashmansworth **2**; North Baddesley; Baughurst **3**; Binstead (IoW) **21**; Bishopstoke; Bishops Waltham; Braishfield; Brambridge; Bramshaw (diocese of Salisbury) **12**; Brickmerston **15**; Brighstone (IoW) **20**; Brockhampton *17*; Burghclere **2**; Bursash **15**; Bursledon **13**; Cadlands **15**; Calbourne (IoW) **20**; Catisfield **16**; Charlecott **6**; Cheriton; Chilbolton **9**; Chilcombe; Combe (nr. Petersfield); Compton; Cranborne **9**; Crawley **9**; Dean (nr. Fareham) **16**; Denmead; Droxford; Durley; Easton; Exbury **15**; Exton; Fareham **16**; Fawley **15**; Freefolk **6**; Frensham (arch. of Surrey) **8**; Froxfield; Gosport **18**; Hamble **13**; Hambledon; Hannington **4**; Harbridge **14**; Hardley **15**; Havant **17**; Highclere **2**; Hill; Hoe; Holbury **15**; Holdenhurst **19**; Houghton **10**; Hunton **9**; Hursley; Hurstbourne Priors **6**; Hythe **15**; Kilmeston; Langley **15**; Leigh **17**; Lepe **15**; Littleton **9**; Medstead; Meonstoke; East and West Meon; Merdon; Michelmersh; Midlington; Morestead; Newtown (IoW); Otterbourne; Overton **5**; Ovington; Ower **15**; Owslebury; Oxenbourne; Polhampton **5**; Privett; Ramsdean; Ringwood **14**; St.Mary Bourne **6**, Shamblehurst; Shedfield; Silkstead; Soberton; Stanswood **15**; Steep; Stone **15**; South Stoneham; Stratfield Mortimer (archd. of Berks, dioc. of Salisbury) **1**; Sutton Scotney **9**; Swanmore; Tadley **3**; Tichborne; Twyford; Upham; Bishops Waltham; North Waltham **7**; Warnford; Whitchurch **6**; Winchester St.Cross or St. Faith; Winnall; Wonston **9**; East Woodhay **2**.

HAMPSHIRE and the ISLE of WIGHT
(Bournemouth area now in Dorset; Isle of Wight now a separate county)

Since 1858: Probate records for England and Wales are at the *Principal Registry of the Family Division, Somerset House, Strand, London WC2R 1LP.* Indexes to these to 1935 are held locally at the *Hampshire Record Office, Winchester;* viewable on microfiche. This microfiche edition of the national indexes is also available for sale, enquiries direct to Hampshire R.O. For other copies see page 11.

Registered copy wills proved at Winchester, 1858-1943 (to 1926 for Hampshire only) are deposited at the *Hampshire Record Office* and are partially indexed.

Before 1858: Hampshire (including the Isle of Wight) was in the province of Canterbury and the diocese of Winchester.

Apart from P.C.C. (see page 12 and right), all probate records for the county are at the

Hampshire Record Office, *Winchester*

which issues a free leaflet *Getting Started at Hampshire Record Office: Wills.*

There are two indexes to cover the four main series of records (Consistory Court wills, Archdeaconry of Winchester Court wills, Peculiar Courts wills, Consistory Court admons):

1. **Pre-1570.** All wills: personal and place names, occupations, TS.
2. **1571-1858.** All wills, admons., invs: personal and place names, occupations. Computer based, on microfiche. Microfiche on sale at £15.

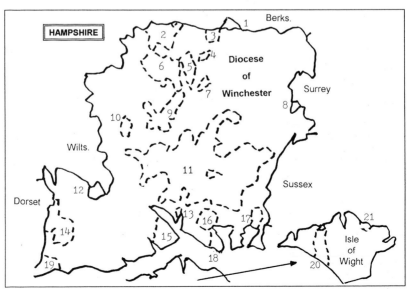

Hampshire continued

Printed index: *Wills, Administrations and Inventories with the Winchester Diocesan Records*, A.J. Willis, 1968. This is of a small collection, now at the *Hampshire R.O.*, mainly Consistory (**1617-1640**) and Archdeaconry (**1617-1626**).

TS copies of calendars, **Consistory** wills **1502-1857**, **Archdeaconry** wills **1502-1792** (all now superseded by recently completed indexes at *Hampshire R.O.*); also MS list of Hampshire wills in **P.C.C 1671-1734**, by H.A. Pitman; all at the *Society of Genealogists*.

HEREFORDSHIRE
(now part of Hereford and Worcester)

Since 1858: Probate records for England and Wales are at the *Principal Registry of the Family Division, Somerset House, Strand, London WC2R 1LP*. Indexes to these (to 1929) are held locally at the *Glos. Record Office*; see also page 11. Registered copy wills proved at Hereford (for Herefordshire), 1858-1928, are deposited at the *National Library of Wales, Aberystwyth*, and are indexed.

Before 1858: Herefordshire was in the province of Canterbury and diocese of Hereford.

Apart from P.C.C. (page 12) probate records for most of the county are at the

Record Office, Hereford.

The main collections are for the **Episcopal Consistory Court of Hereford**, which covered most of the county, and the **Consistory Court of the Dean of Hereford**, which included Hereford itself and 25 nearby parishes (listed right). Card index to wills in both courts, **1600-1660**. Chronological list to Episcopal-Consistory Court wills and invs **1539-99**, invs **1628-1641**. After **1660**, to **1857**, indexes in act books to wills and admons for both courts.

Also, three peculiars:

Little Hereford (Heref.) and **Ashford Carbonell** (Salop), from **1662**;
Upper Bullinghope or **Bullingham**, from **1675**;
Moreton Magna or **Moreton on Lugg**, from **1668** (all indexed).

A consolidated index to all records in the two consistory courts and three peculiars to **1700** is in preparation for publication by the *BRS*.

BRS has already published, as *Microfiche 2*, a Calendar of Probate and Admon Acts 1407-1581 and abstracts of Wills 1541-1581 in Court Books of the Bishop of Hereford. The wills they refer to are no longer extant.

Eight parishes in the south-west of the county were in the **Archdeaconry of Brecon** (diocese of St. David's). Records at the *National Library of Wales*, page 66.

Herefordshire continued

Parishes in the **Consistory of the Dean of Hereford (D):**
Allensmore; Blakemore; Breinton; Brockhampton **7**; Canon Pyon **2**; Clehonger; Dewsall **8**; Dinedor; Eaton Bishop; Hampton Bishop; Hereford; Holmer; Huntingdon; Kingstone; Madley; Mardon; Moreton Jeffreys **3**; Norton Canon **4**; Pipe; Preston on Wye; Preston Wynne; Putley **7**; Thruxton; Tyberton; Withington; Woolhope **7**.

Archdeaconry of Brecon (B):
Clodock; Dulas; Michaelchurch Escley; Ewyas Harold; Llancillo; St. Margaret; Rowlston; Walterstone; Fwddog, **9**.

Peculiars:
Little Hereford **1**; Moreton on Lugg **5**; Bullingham **6**.

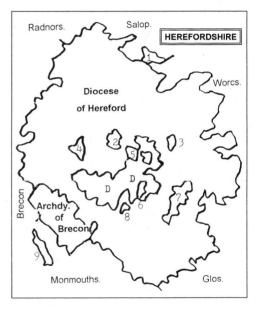

HERTFORDSHIRE

Since 1858: Probate records for England and Wales are at the *Principal Registry of the Family Division, Somerset House, Strand, London WC2R 1LP.* In addition to Somerset House, a copy of the index is available locally at the *Huntingdon branch of the Cambridgeshire Record Office.* For other copies, see page 11.

Before 1858: Hertfordshire was in the province of Canterbury - for records of P.C.C., see page 12.

Apart from P.C.C., probate records for most of the country are at the

> **Hertfordshire Record Office,** *Hertford*

(see guide, *Genealogical Sources*).

Except for parishes on the eastern border (see below), the county was in the intermingled jurisdictions of the **Archdeaconry of St. Albans** (diocese of London) (mainly SW corner) and the **Archdeaconry of Huntingdon (Hitchin Division)** (diocese of Lincoln). All probate records held at *Hertfordshire R.O.* for these two courts are in a consolidated card index (**St. Albans**, wills from **1415**, admons from **1540**; **Huntingdon**, wills from **1557**, admons from **1610**). Printed index to wills and admons in **Hitchin Division** act books, **1566-1573, 1596-1599** (*BRS 42*, pp. 210-16).

Transcripts of all (303) wills proved in the Court of the Archdeacon of St. Albans in *St. Albans Wills 1471-1500,* ed. Susan Flood, Herts R.S., 1994.

Until **1609**, most records for the **Archdeaconry of Huntingdon** (the major part of the county) are at the

> **County Record Office,** *Huntingdon*

(see *Genealogical Sources in Cambridgeshire,* 2nd edn., 1994). Printed index, wills **1479-1609**, admons **1559-1609** (*BRS 42*).

Eastern border parishes (31 listed right) were in the **Archdeaconry Court of Middlesex** and **Commissary Court of London (Essex and Herts Division),** records at

> **Essex Record Office,** *Chelmsford.*

Printed indexes, wills **1431-1857** (*BRS 78, 79* and *84*). MS calendars to admons, **Commissary** from **1691**; **Archdeaconry** from **1660**.

The **Consistory Court of London** had concurrent jurisdiction with the Archdeaconries of St. Albans and Middlesex, so some Herts. testators are to be found amongst the records of this court, at

> **London Metropolitan Archives** (formerly *G.L.R.O.*) (see page 36).

Calendar from **1514**, and index in preparation (to 1719) for publication by *BRS.*

The parishes of Albury, Brent Pelham and Furneux Pelham were in the **Peculiar of the Dean and Chapter of St. Paul's,** records at the

> **Guildhall Library,** *London* (see page 36):

wills **1560-1837** (card index to Herts. testators at *Herts. R.O.*), admons **1646-1837** (calendar). Full index in preparation for publication by *BRS.*

Places in the east of Hertfordshire in the jurisdiction of the Archdeaconry of Middlesex Commissary Court of London (Essex and Herts divisions) (diocese of London); and the Peculiar Court of the Dean and Chapter of St. Paul's (**P**):

Albury (**P**); Gt. Amwell; Anstey; Barkway; Barley; Braughing; Brent Pelham (**P**); Broxbourne; Buckland; Cheshunt; Eastwick; Furneux Pelham (**P**); Gilston; Much and Little Hadham; Hoddesdon; Gt. and Little Hormead; Hunsdon; Layston; Meesden; Reed; Royston; Sawbridgeworth; Standon; Stanstead Abbots; Stanstead St. Margarets; Stocking Pelham; Bishops Stortford; Thorley; Thundridge; Ware; Widford; Wormley; Wyddial.

Archdeaconry of Bedford (diocese of Lincoln):

Caddington (**1**)   Studham (**2**)

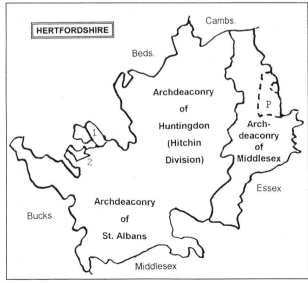

HUNTINGDONSHIRE
(now part of Cambridgeshire)

See *Genealogical Sources in Cambridgeshire* by Michael Farrar, Cambridgeshire Record Office, 2nd edition, 1994.

Since 1858: Probate records for England and Wales are at the *Principal Registry of the Family Division, Somerset House, Strand, London WC2R 1LP.* Indexes to these (to 1966) are held locally at the *County Record Office (Cambridgeshire C.C.), Cambridge.* For other copies, see page 11.

Registered copies of Huntingdonshire wills proved at Peterborough, 1858-1941 are at the *Northamptonshire Record Office, Northampton,* and are indexed.

Before 1858: Huntingdonshire was in the province of Canterbury and formed the Archdeaconry of Huntingdon in the diocese of Lincoln.

Apart from P.C.C. (see page 12) probate records for virtually the whole county are at the

County Record Office, *Huntingdon*

(part of *Cambridgeshire Record Office*).

Except for a few places (see below) the county was entirely within the jurisdiction of the **Commissary Court of the Bishop of Lincoln and of the Archdeacon in the Archdeaconry of Huntingdon.** Printed index: wills **1479-1652**, admons **1559-1614** *(BRS 42).* MS index, wills **1615-1857**, admons **1662-1688**; MS calendar, admons **1691-1857**.

Peculiars:
Brampton 1549-1855;
Buckden 1661-1855;
Stow Longa (incl. Barham, Little Catworth, Easton and Spaldwick) **1661-1857;**
Leighton Bromswold 1738-1838.
Printed index: *Trans. Cambs. & Hunts. Arch. Soc.*, 6, pt.3, pp. 76-96. Buckden and Stow Longa are also partially indexed in *BRS 57.*

Exceptions:
Washingley, in the **Consistory Court of Peterborough**, see page 40.

Records for places in the Peculiars of Stow Longa and Leighton Bromswold may also be found in the **Peculiar Court of the Dean and Chapter of Lincoln**, see page 35.

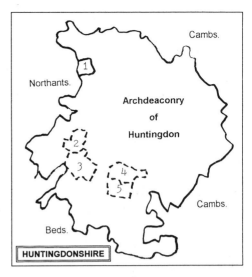

Archdeaconry of Huntingdon

Cambs.

Northants.

Beds.

Cambs.

HUNTINGDONSHIRE

Places outside the jurisdiction of the archdeaconry court:

Brampton (**4**); Buckden (**5**); Leighton Bromswold (**2**); Stow Longa with Little Catworth, Easton and Spaldwick (**3**); Washingley (**1**).

KENT
(See *A Guide to Sources for Family History*, Kent County Archives Office.)

Since 1858: Probate records for England and Wales are at the *Principal Registry of the Family Division, Somerset House, Strand, London WC2R 1LP.* Indexes to these (over 50 years old) are held locally at the *East Sussex Record Office, Lewes;* for other copies, see page 11.

Before 1858: Kent was in the province of Canterbury - for records of P.C.C. see page 12.

Apart from P.C.C., probate records for most of the county are at the

Centre for Kentish Studies, *Maidstone.*

The county comprised the two dioceses of Canterbury and Rochester.

Eastern Kent was in the **Diocese of Canterbury.** Jurisdiction of **Consistory** and **Archdeaconry** courts was intermingled and overlapping, so indexes to both courts should be examined.

Printed indexes: wills and admons **1396-1577** *(BRS **50, 65**);* **1640-1650** *(BRS 50).* Calendars (separate for each court), wills and admons **1578-1857** (indexing in progress for publication by *BRS).*

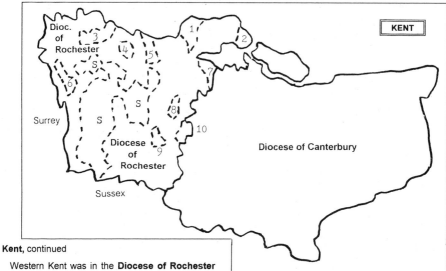

KENT

Surrey

Dioc.
of
Rochester

Diocese
of
Rochester

Sussex

Diocese of Canterbury

Kent, continued

Western Kent was in the **Diocese of Rochester** (apart from the Deanery of Shoreham, below). Jurisdiction of **Consistory** and **Archdeaconry Courts** was concurrent. Printed index: wills and admons **1440-1561** *(Kent A.S. 9)* (Consistory only). Consolidated card index, wills only, to both courts, **1498-1857** (noticeable decline in business from *c.*1750). Calendars to admons from **1562**.

In western Kent 38 parishes were in the **Peculiar of the Deanery of Shoreham**. Original records are now at the *Lambeth Palace Library, London* but the *Centre for Kentish Studies* has all these on microfilm.
Indexes: wills and admons **1614-1821, 1841** (C19 calendar; also TS index at *SofG*). Later records appear to be missing. See *Sevenoaks Wills and Inventories in the Reign of Charles II, Kent Archaeological Society (Kent Records) 25* (1988).
Peculiar of Cliffe (that parish only). Index: all records **1671-1845**. See also Rochester card index.
After 1846 records for the parishes of Charlton, Deptford, Eltham, Greenwich, Lee, Lewisham, Plumstead and Woolwich should be found in the **Consistory Court of London** at *London Metropolitan Archives* (formerly *G.L.R.O.*).

Peculiar Deanery of Shoreham (**S**):

Bexley **3**; Brasted; Chevening; Chiddingstone; St. Mary Cray; Crayford **3**; Darenth **4**; Downe **6**; Eynsford; East Farleigh **10**; Farningham; Gillingham **7**; Grain **2**; Halstead; Hayes; Hever; Hunton **10**; Ide Hill; Ifield; Ightham; Keston **6**; Knockholt; Lidsing; East Malling **8**; Meopham; Northfleet **5**; Orpington; Otford; East Peckham **9**; Penshurst; Plaxtol; Sevenoaks; Shoreham; Stanstead; Sundridge; Wrotham.
Peculiar of Cliffe (at Hoo) - **1**.

LANCASHIRE
(now split between the counties of Lancashire, Greater Manchester and Merseyside; Furness now in Cumbria and southern border area in Cheshire.)

See *Finding Folk: A Handlist of Genealogical Sources*, Lancashire R.O., 10th edition, 1995 (£8.50 + p&p).

Since 1858: Probate records for England and Wales are at the *Principal Registry of the Family Division, Somerset House, Strand, London WC2R 1LP*. Indexes to these are held locally by the *Lancashire Record Office, Preston* (to 1966); the *Liverpool Record Office* (to 1928); and the *Greater Manchester County Record Office*. For other copies, see page 11.
Registered copy wills proved at Lancaster, 1858-1940 (until 1926 confined to Lancashire excl. Manchester, Salford and Hundred of West Derby) and Liverpool (Hundred of West Derby) (many damaged), 1858-1940, are deposited at the *Lancashire Record Office, Preston*.

Lancashire continued

Before 1858: Lancashire was in the province of York - for records of P.C.Y., see page 56; and also records of P.C.C., page 12. Printed index: *Lancs. wills and admons in P.C.C., 1650-1660 (Lancs. & Cheshire R.S. 4*, pp. 250-300).

Apart from P.C.Y. and P.C.C. nearly all probate records for the county are held at the

> ### Lancashire Record Office, *Preston*.

The county was in the diocese of Chester, but records for the archdeaconry of Richmond (north of the Ribble) are generally separate.

For the **Consistory Court of Chester** there are indexes published by *Lancs. and Cheshire Record Soc.* to wills and admons, **1545-1837**, with the prospect of further volumes to come.

Meanwhile there is a card index to the remaining years, 1838-1857 (A-G also in typescript).

In this diocese only, estates worth less than £40 were kept in a separate 'infra' series, and, in the published index volumes, are in a separate volume before 1665, and in appendices from 1660 to 1800. Since 1800 they have been indexed jointly with the main series. To 1820 Cheshire and Lancashire wills and admons are intermingled, but from 1821 they are in separate sections in each volume.

Lancashire & Cheshire Rec. Soc vols and dates:
1545-1650 (main series) *2* and *4;*
1590-1665 ('infra' series) *52;*
1660-1800 *15, 18, 20, 22, 25, 37, 38, 44, 45;*
1801-1820 *62, 63 , 78;*
1821-1837 (Lancs separate) *107, 113, 118, 120.*

Vols *33, 43, 52* list miscellaneous wills **1487-1800**; and additional wills and admons for **1670** and **1692** are in vol *63*.

The county north of the River Ribble lay in the **Archdeaconry of Richmond (Western Deaneries).** The *Lancs. and Ches. Record Soc* has published indexes to all the Lancashire records **1457-1857** vols *10, 13, 23, 66, 99*, and *105*. *Cumbria Record Office, Kendal*, has m'f of wills for the Deaneries of Furness, **1538-1860**, and Amounder-ness, **1748-1858**.

Manorial Court of Halton (parish of Halton only): printed index: wills and admons **1615-1815**, *L&CRS 23, 66, 99*.

In addition to P.C.Y. (above) there are a few Lancashire wills at the *Borthwick Institute, York,* for Aighton, Chaigley and Bailey, in the **Exchequer Court of York** (page 56), and for Broughton, Kirkby Ireleth and Seathwaite (Furness) in the **Peculiar Court of the Dean and Chapter of York** and occasionally in the **Chancery Court of York**) (page 56).

Rochdale Public Library has a big collection of abstracts of wills and admons relating to Rochdale people, 1553-1810.

Peculiar of the Dean and Chapter of York (1):
Broughton, Kirkby Ireleth, Seathwaite.

Manor of Halton (2):

Diocese of York (3):
Aighton, Bailey, Chaigley.

There is an index to **Colne** wills, **1545-1830**, at *Colne Library.*

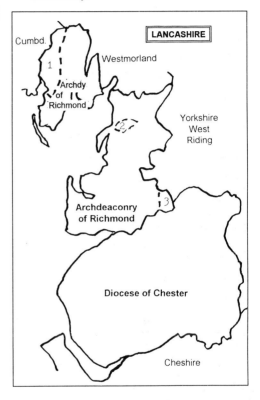

LEICESTERSHIRE

Since 1858: Probate records for England and Wales are at the *Principal Registry of the Family Division, Somerset House, Strand, London WC2R 1LP.* Indexes to these held locally in Leicester will be transferred over a period from the *District Probate Registry, Leicester* to the *Leicestershire Record Office.* There is also a set at the *Nottinghamshire Record Office.* For other copies, see page 11.

Registered copy wills proved at Leicester, 1858-1940 (to 1926 for Leicestershire only) are deposited at the *Leicestershire Record Office* (card index to 1918). Original wills, 1858-1969, are still held at the *Leicester District Probate Registry.*

Places outside the jurisdiction of the archdeaconry of Leicester:

Manor of Rothley:
Barsby **3**; Chadwell **1**; South Croxton **3**; Gaddesby **3**; Grimston **2**; Keyham **8**; Mountsorrel **4**; Rothley **4**; Saxelby **2**; Somerby **5**; Wartnaby **2**; Wycomb **1**.

Peculiar of Groby:
Anstey **6**; Bradgate Park **6**; Charnwood Forest **6**; Cropston **6**; Glenfield **6**; Hallgate **6**; Newton Linford **6**; Ratby **6**; Swanton under Bardon **7**; Swithland **6**.

Manor of Evington - 6

Prebend of St. Margaret, Leicester - 10:
Knighton; Leicester St. Margaret.

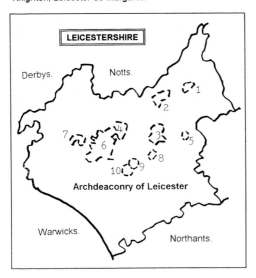

Archdeaconry of Leicester

Before 1858: Leicestershire was in the province of Canterbury and formed the archdeaconry of Leicester in the diocese of Lincoln.

Apart from P.C.C (see page 12) all probate records for the county are at

Leicestershire Record Office, *Wigston Magna*

which issues an information sheet (no. **5**) *How to Trace your Family.*

For the **Archdeaconry of Leicester** there are printed indexes to wills, **1495-1750**, and admons, **1556-1750** *(BRS 27, 51)* and a consolidated card index to all records, **1751-1857.**

BRS **27** and **51** also print indexes to the four peculiars:

St. Margaret in Leicester: 1543-1800
Manor of Rothley: 1575-1800
Manor of Evington: 1581-1800
Peculiar of Groby: 1580, 1636-1637, 1670-1800

Wills and admons for **1801-1857** are included in the main card index.

The *Leicestershire Record Office* also has a large collection of Leicester will abstracts, **1563-1800.**

LINCOLNSHIRE
(northern border now in Humberside)

Since 1858: Probate records for England and Wales are at the *Principal Registry of the Family Division, Somerset House, Strand, London WC2R 1LP.* Indexes to these are held locally at *Lincolnshire Archives,* 1858-1935. Post-1935 indexes are at the *Lincoln Probate Sub-Registry, Lincoln.* For other copies, see page 11.

Registered copy wills proved at Lincoln (for Lincolnshire), 1858-1941, are deposited at *Lincolnshire Archives,* indexed to 1874 only. Original wills are at *Lincoln Probate Sub-Registry.*

Before 1858: Lincolnshire was in the province of Canterbury and diocese of Lincoln. Nevertheless see also P.C.Y. (right and pages 56-57).

Apart from P.C.C. (see page 12) and P.C.Y., probate records for the whole county are at the

Lincolnshire Archives, *Lincoln*

which issues a leaflet on records for the family historian.

Lincolnshire continued

Most of the county was in the jurisdiction of the **Consistory Court of Lincoln** (the whole county from 1834). There are printed indexes to wills **1506-1653** *(BRS 28, 41)*, **1660-1700** *(BRS 101)*, admons **1540-1659** *(BRS 52)* and invs **1660-1700** *(BRS 101)*; a typed index to wills **1701-1750**, and MS calendars to wills **1751-1857**, admons **1660-1857**; invs **1504-1653, 1701-1831**.

Until 1834 the **Archdeaconry of Stow** had separate jurisdiction over 78 parishes in the north-west of the county. There is a printed index to wills **1530-1699** and admons **1580-1699** in *BRS 57*; and MS calendars **1700-1834**; MS list of invs **1616-1787**.

There are printed indexes to wills, admons and invs for the complete period for all **Peculiars** in the county in *BRS 57*. Of these the **Peculiar of the Dean and Chapter of Lincoln** includes 25 parishes **(1534-1834)**. The others are **Caistor (1636-1833), Corringham (1632-1833), Heydour (1669-1836), Kirton-in-Lindsey (1535-1834), Louth (1612-1857), Bishop Norton (1613-1814), Sleaford (1610-1834)** and **Stow in Lindsey (1549-1833)**. Records for all except Louth became merged with the Consistory from about 1834.

The *Society of Genealogists* has a TS index to Lincs. wills and admons **1731-1857** in P.C.York.

Will abstracts, **1271-1532**, published in *Lincoln Record Soc.* vols. *5, 10, 24.*
Probate Invs. of Lincoln Citizens 1661-1714, ed. J.A. Johnston, *Lincoln Record Soc. 80.*

Parishes and places in the direct jurisdiction of the consistory court, i.e., in the archdeaconry of Stow or in one of the following peculiars; **Dean and Chapter of Lincoln (D); Caistor (CA); Corringham (CO); Heydour (H); Kirton in Lindsey (K); Louth (L); Bishop Norton (BN); Sleaford** or **Lafford (SL); and Stow in Lindsey (ST).**

Aisby in Corringham **CO6**; Aisby in Heydour **H24**; Aisthorpe, Alkborough; Althorpe; Appleby; Asgarby **D20**; Atterby **BN7**; Audleby **CA4**; Barlings; Belton in Axholme; Binbrook **D9**, Blyborough; Blyton; Bottesford; Bransby **ST14**; Brattleby; Broughton; Broxholme; Burton by Lincoln; Burton on Stather; Buslingthorpe; Caenby; Caistor **CA4**; Cammeringham; North and South Carlton **D15**; Cherry Willingham; Clixby **CA4**; Coates; Cold Hanworth; Corringham **CO6**; Crowle; Culverthorpe **H24**; Dalby **D19**; Dunholme **D13**; Dunstall **CO6**, Epworth; Faldingworth; Fenton; Fillingham; East Firsby; Fiskerton; Flixborough; Fonaby **CA4**; Friesthorpe **D12**; Frodingham; Gainsborough; Glentham **D8**; Glentworth; Grayingham; Greetwell; Hackthorne; Hainton **D11**; West Halton; Harpswell; Haxey; Heapham; Hemswell; Heydour **H24**; Hibaldstow **D2**; Holdingham **SL23**; Holton le Moor **CA4**; Huckerby **CO6**; Hundon **CA4**; Ingham; Kelby **H24**; North Kelsey **D3**; Kettlethorpe, Kirton in Lindsey **K5**; Knaith; Laughton; Lea; Lincoln St. John. St. Margaret, St. Mary Magd. and St. Nicholas **D18**; Louth **L10**; Luddington; Manton; Marton; Melton Ross **D1**; Messingham; Nettleham; Newton on Trent; Normanby; Normanby by Stow **ST14**; Northorpe **CO6**; Bishop Norton **BN7**; Oasby **H24**; Owmby by Spital; Owston; Redbourne; Reepham; Roxby with Risby; Saxby St. Helen; Saxilby; Scamblesby **D17**; Scampton; Scawby; Scothorne; Scotter; Scotton; Scredington **D25**; Searby cum Owmby **D3**; Skillington **D26**; Sleaford **SL23**; Snarford; Snitterby; Somerby **CO6**; Southrey in p. Bardney **D**; Spital in the Street **BN7**; Spridlington; Springthorpe; Stow in Lindsey **ST14**; Strubby **D16**; Sturton **ST14**; Sudbrooke; Thurlby **D21**; Torksey; Upton; Waddingham; Wellingore **D22**; Welton by Lincoln **D13**; Whitton; Willingham; Willoughton; Winteringham; Winterton; Wroot; Yawthorpe **CO6**.

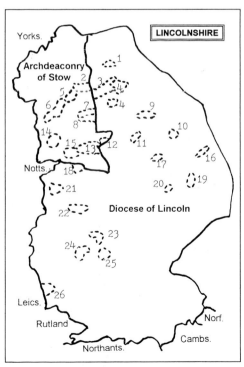

Yorks.

LINCOLNSHIRE

Archdeaconry of Stow

Notts.

Diocese of Lincoln

Leics.

Rutland

Northants.

Norf.

Cambs.

LONDON and MIDDLESEX

Since 1858: Probate records for England and Wales are at the *Principal Registry of the Family Division, Somerset House, Strand, London WC2R 1LP.* For copies of the index elsewhere, see p. 11.

Before 1858: The city of London and county of Middlesex were in the province of Canterbury and diocese of London. The various jurisdictions are probably more complicated than anywhere else in the country and the searcher is advised to examine all major courts, split though they are between several record offices. P.C.C. was greatly used.

There is a **London Probate Index, 1750-1858,** to wills and admons (taken from the calendars) for *all* courts except the P.C.C.:
1. 1837-1858, complete.
2. 1750-1800, nearing completion (open late 1994).
3. 1801-1836, in progress, not open for enquiries.
   Enquiries to *David Wright, 71 Island Wall, Whitstable, Kent CT5 1EL;* £5 for up to 10 entries of a surname, 50p per entry threafter.

London Metropolitan Archives (formerly G.L.R.O.), 40 Northampton Rd, London EC1R 0AB.

Consistory Court of London. The superior court, with jurisdiction over the whole city and the county except peculiars, so it should always be searched in addition to others listed below. Records include those of the Diocese of Westminster, 1541-1550 (other records for these years are at *Westminster City Archives*). Indexes are in preparation for publication by *BRS*, 1492-1719; meanwhile calendars, partly 19th cent, remain in use, 1492, 1508, **1514-1857.**

Archdeaconry of Middlesex (Middlesex Division). Jurisdiction over 26 parishes in Middlesex (see list, right). Wills **1608-1612, 1662-1701,** admons **1667-1701** (19th cent MS calendar; full index in preparation for publication by *BRS*); wills **1702-1736** (card index, and in progress); wills **1737-1794, 1799,** admons **1702-1760** (19th cent MS calendar); invs **1667-1773** (card index).

Guildhall Library, Aldermanbury, EC2P 2EJ.

See *Guide to the London Collections,* 1978; and *A Guide to Genealogical Sources in the Guildhall Library,* 2nd edn.

Commissary Court of London (London Division). Jurisdiction over about half the parishes both in the city and in the county. Printed index, wills and admons **1374-1625** *(BRS 82, 86, 97),* **1626-1649, 1661-1700,** Pt 1, **A-G** *(BRS 102),* **H-S** *(BRS 108),* T-Z (part 3 for publication by *BRS*). Wills and admons **1571-1629** (modern MS index in short periods); **1629-1857** (MS calendar).

Archdeaconry of London. Jurisdiction over about 40 parishes in the city and 3 populous parishes bordering it; incl. St. Botolph Aldgate, to which many mariners, dying abroad, were ascribed as residents (otherwise see P.C.C.).

Archdeaconry of London ctd: Printed index, wills **1393-1421, 1524-1649, 1661-1700,** admons **1564-1649, 1661-1700** *(BRS 89, 98).* Wills and admons **1701-1781** (a few to 1807), pub. Soc. of Gen.

Peculiar of the Dean and Chapter St. Paul's Cathedral. Jurisdiction over 4 parishes in the city and all or parts of 10 in the county. Wills **1535-1672** (MS 19th cent index); wills **1672-1837,** admons **1646-1837** (calendars). New index in preparation for publication by *BRS*.

Royal Peculiar of St. Katherine by the Tower. Wills **1689-1772, 1818,** admons **1688-1793** (TS, for publication by *BRS*).

Corporation of London Record Office, Guildhall, London EC2P 2EJ.

Court of Husting. The court of the corporation of the city of London, with jurisdiction in the city and liberties, to 1688 only. Printed index and abstracts, wills **1258-1688** *(Calendar of Wills ...in the Court of Husting,* R.R. Sharpe, 2 vols, 1888-9; facsimile on microfiche, 1252-1485, Chadwyck Healey).

Lambeth Palace Library, London SE1 7JU.

Deanery of the Arches (Peculiar of the Archbishop of Canterbury). Jurisdiction in thirteen city parishes (only). Wills, admons and invs, **1620-1780, 1832** *(BRS 98).*

Deanery of Croydon (Peculiar of the Archbishop of Canterbury). Jurisdiction incl. Middlesex parishes of Harrow with Pinner and Hayes with Norwood. Wills, admons and invs **1602-1832** (19th cent MS index, also TS at *P.R.O.* and *S of G).*

City of Westminster Archives Centre, 10 St. Ann's Street, London SW1P 2XR.

Royal Peculiar of the Dean and Chapter of Westminster (pre-1539 **Abbot of Westminster).** Jurisdiction, Precincts of the Abbey, St. Margaret Westminster until 1829 (including St. John the Evangelist from 1728); part of St. Martin in the Fields until late C17; Paddington until c.1669 (from c.1700 see under consistory of London and archdeaconry of Middlesex); precincts of St. Martin le Grand (until 1829), and parts of parishes of St. Leonard Foster Lane (until c.1670), and St. Anne and St. Agnes within Aldersgate (until c.1670); for Essex parishes in the Peculiar see page 36).

Wills and admons **1504-1700** (printed in *Indexes to the Ancient Testamentary Records of Westminster,* A.M. Burke, 1913; incl. Westminster wills and admons in Consistory, 1540-1556 (in *GLRO),* and miscellaneous testamentary records, 1228-1700, (in *Westminster Abbey Muniment Room*); also, as above, and to **1820/30** (very few in later period) (printed calendar, 1864, never published; another copy at *P.R.O.,* but very few other copies are known to exist).

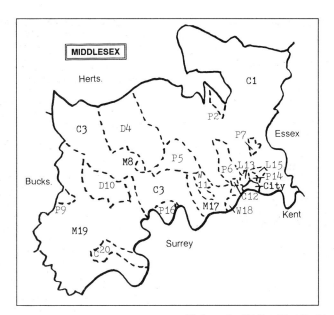

The parishes and chapelries in the city of London and the county of Middlesex are listed below, with the jurisdiction(s) into which they fell indicated as follows:

C: Commissary Court of London (London division); **L:** Archdeaconry of London; **M:** Archdeaconry of Middlesex; **A:** Peculiar Deanery of the Arches; **D:** Peculiar Deanery of Croydon; **P:** Peculiar of the Dean and Chapter of St. Paul's; **K:** Peculiar of St. Katherine-by-the-Tower; **W:** Peculiar of the Dean and Chapter of Westminster; **S:** Archdeaconry Court of Surrey (diocese of Winchester) - parishes in Southwark were still in that county in 1858 (see page 49).

Numbers refer to the map.

This list is based, for the city, on that in Lewis's *Topographical Dictionary* published in 1831, and includes places that may have been chapelries within other parishes and subsequently became parishes in their own right. Parishes were in the city or in its immediate vicinity unless otherwise stated.

Acton **C3**; St. Alban Wood Street **C**; Allhallows Barking **C**; Allhallows the Great **L**; Allhallows Honey Lane **C**; Allhallows the Less **L;** Allhallows Lombard Street **A**; Allhallows Staining **C**; Allhallows London Wall and St. Augustin Papey **L**; St. Alphage London Wall **L**; St. Andrew Holborn **L13**; St. Andrew Hubbard **C**; St. Andrew Undershaft with St. Mary Axe **C**; St. Andrew-by-the-Wardrobe **L**; St. Anne and St. Agnes Aldersgate with St. John Zachary **W & L**; St. Anne Blackfriars **C**; St. Anne (Soho) Westminster **M**; St. Antholin **C**; Ashford **M19**;

St. Augustine Watling Street **L**; Friern Barnet **P2**; St. Bartholomew by the Exchange **L**; St. Bartholomew the Great **L**; St. Bartholomew the Less **L**; Bedfont **M19**; St. Benet Fink **C**; St. Benet Gracechurch **C**; St. Benet Paul's Wharf **C**; St. Benet Sherehog **C**; Bethnal Green, St. Matthew **C1**; St. Botolph Aldersgate **L**; St. Botolph Aldgate **L**; St. Botolph Billingsgate **C**; St. Botolph without Bishopsgate **C**, Bow **C**, Brentford **M19**, St. Bride, Fleet Street **C**; Bromley St. Leonard **C1**; Chelsea **M17**; Chiswick **P16**; Christchurch Greyfriars Newgate Street **L**; Christchurch Southwark **S**; Christchurch Spitalfields **C1**; St. Christopher le Stocks **C**; St. Clement Danes **M**; St. Clement Eastcheap **C**; Cowley **M19**; Cranford **M19**; St. Dionis Backchurch **A**; West Drayton **P9**; St. Dunstan in the East **A**; St. Dunstan in the West **C3**; Edgware **C1**; Edmonton **C1**; St. Edmund the King **C**; Enfield **C1**; St. Ethelburga **L**; St. Faith **P**; Feltham **M19**; Finchley **C1**; Fulham **C3**; St. Gabriel Fenchurch **C**; St. George Bloomsbury **C12**; St. George Botolph Lane **C**; St. George in the East **C1**; St. George Hanover Square **M17**; St. George the Martyr and St. Andrew above Bars **L13;** St. George Southwark **S**; St. Giles Cripplegate **P**; St. Giles in the Fields **C12**; St. Gregory by St. Paul's **P**; Greenford **C3**; Hackney **C1**; Monken Hadley or Hadleigh **C1**; Hammersmith **C3**; Hampstead **C1**; Hampton **M19**; Hanwell **M19**; Hanworth **C20**; Harefield **C3**; Harlington **M19**; Harmondsworth **M19**; Harrow **D4**; Hayes **D10**; St. Helen Bishopsgate **P**; Hendon **C1**; Heston **M19**; Highgate **P6**; Hillingdon **M19**; Hornsey **C1**; Hounslow **M19**; Hoxton (Shoreditch) **P**; Ickenham **C3**; Isleworth **M19**;

London and Middlesex, continued

Islington **C1**; St. James Clerkenwell **L13**; St. James Duke's Place **C**; St. James Garlickhythe **C**; St. James (Piccadilly) Westminster **M**; St. John Baptist **L**; St. John Baptist Savoy **L**; St. John Clerkenwell **L13**; St. John Evangelist Watling Street **A**; St. John Evangelist Westminster **W18**; St. John Horsleydown **S**; St. John Millbank (Smith Square) **C**; St. John Zachary **L**; St. Katherine Coleman **L**; St.Katherine Creechurch **C**; St. Katherine by the Tower **K**; Kensington **M17**; Kingsbury **C1**; Laleham **M19**; St. Lawrence Jewry **C**; St. Lawrence Pountney **C**; St. Leonard Eastcheap **A**; St. Leonard Foster **W &** **C**; St. Leonard Shoreditch **L15**; Limehouse **C1**; Littleton **M19**; St. Luke Old Street **P14**; St. Magnus the Martyr **L**; St. Margaret New Fish Street **C**; St. Margaret Lothbury **L**; St. Margaret Moses **L**; St. Margaret Pattens **C**; St. Margaret Westminster **M & W 18**; St. Martin in the Fields **W & L**; Precincts of St. Martin-le-Grand **W**; St. Martin Ironmonger Lane **C**; St. Martin Ludgate **L**; St. Martin Orgar **C**; St. Martin Outwich **C**; St. Martin Vintry **C**; St. Mary Abchurch **L**; St. Mary Aldermanbury **C**; St. Mary Aldermary **A**; St. Mary-le-bone **C1**; St. Mary Bothaw **A**; St. Mary le Bow **A**; St. Mary Colechurch **L**; St. Mary at Hill **L**; St. Mary Magdalene Old Fish Street **L**; St. Mary Magdalene Milk Street **C**; St. Mary Mounthaw **L**; St. Mary Somerset **L**: St. Mary Staining **L**; St. Mary le Strand **M**; St. Mary Woolchurch Haw **C**; St. Mary Woolnoth **L**; St. Matthew Friday Street **C**; St. Michael Bassishaw **L**; St. Michael Cornhill **C**; St. Michael Crooked Lane **A**; St. Michael Queenhithe **L**; St. Michael le Quern **L**; St. Michael Royal **A**; St. Michael Wood Street **C**; St. Mildred Bread Street **C**; St. Mildred Poultry **C**; South Mimms **C1**; St. Nicholas Acons **C**; St. Nicholas Cole Abbey **C**; St. Nicholas Olave **C**; Northolt **C3**; Norwood **D10**; St. Olave Hart Street **L**; St. Olave Old Jewry **C**; St. Olave Silver Street **L**; St. Olave Southwark **S**; Paddington **M & W11**; St. Pancras (Middx) **P6**; St. Pancras Soper Lane **A**; St. Paul Covent Garden **M**; St. Peter Cornhill **L**; St. Peter near St. Paul's Wharf **C**; St. Peter le Poer **C**; St. Peter ad Vincula, Tower*; St. Peter Westcheap **L**; Pinner **D4**; Poplar **C1**; Precinct of Portpool **P**; Ruislip **C3**; St. Saviour Southwark **S**; St. Sepulchre **C**; Shadwell St. Paul **C**; Shepperton **M19**; Shoreditch **P**; Staines **M19**; Stanmore **C1**; Stanwell **M19**; St. Stephen Coleman Street **C**; St. Stephen Walbrook **L**; Stepney **C**; Stoke Newington **P7**; Sunbury **M19**; St. Swithin London Stone **C**; Teddington **C20**; St. Thomas the Apostle **L**; Tottenham **C1**; Trinity the Less **L**; Trinity in the Minories **L**; Twickenham **M19**; Uxbridge **M19**; St. Vedast Foster Lane **A**; Wapping St. John **C**; Precincts of Westminster Abbey **W**; Whitechapel **C1**; Willesden **P5**.

*It is not clear into which court's jurisdiction St. Peter ad Vincula fell.

MONMOUTHSHIRE

See with **South Wales**, pages 65-66.

NORFOLK

Since 1858: Probate records for England and Wales are at the *Principal Registry of the Family Division, Somerset House, Strand, London WC2R 1LP.* Indexes to these (1858-1937) are held locally at the *Norwich Central Library (Norfolk Studies Dept.), Gildengate House, Norwich,* for other copies, see page 11.

Registered copy wills proved at Norwich, 1858-1941, are deposited at the *Norfolk Record Office* and are indexed.

Pre 1858: Norfolk was in the province of Canterbury and the diocese of Norwich. Apart from P.C.C. (see page 12) virtually all probate records for the county are at the

Norfolk Record Office, *Gildengate House, Norwich.*

The Norfolk probate records comprise:

(1) **Consistory Court of Norwich** (jurisdiction throughout the county and diocese including Suffolk and part of Cambridgeshire). Printed indexes to wills, **1370-1603** (*Norfolk Record Soc. 16, 21; BRS 69, 73*), **1604-1857** (*Norfolk R.S. 28, 34, 38, 47*); admons **1371-1646, 1666-1857** (TS indexes); invs **1553-1846** (TS calendar and index).

(2) **Archdeaconry of Norfolk** (jurisdiction: southern Norfolk, and parts of north-eastern and north-western Norfolk, see map and list on right). Printed indexes to wills **1453-1603** (*Norfolk and Norwich Genealogical Soc., 3, 5,* and *10*); TS indexes to wills **1604-1857**; admons **1541-1618, 1661-1857**; TS calendar and index to invs **1728-1774**.

(3) **Archdeaconry of Norwich** (jurisdiction: most of northern Norfolk, and deaneries of Breccles and Thetford in southern Norfolk; see map and list on right). TS indexes to wills **1469-1652, 1660-1857**; admons. **1590-1609, 1624-1637, 1660-1857**; invs **1674-1825**.

(4) **Peculiar of Castle Rising, 1624-1723/4.** Index *Norfolk Genealogy 16.*

(5) **Peculiar of Great Cressingham, 1675-1754.** Index, *Norfolk Genealogy 16.*

(6) **Peculiar of the Dean and Chapter of Norwich** (see map and list for jurisdiction). Wills **1416-1559, 1572-1652, 1660-1857**; admons **1448-1548, 1613-1680, 1737-1857.** Index *Norfolk Genealogy 16* (1985), in two sections, **1444-1600, 1600-1857.** Invs **1681-1782**, index *Norfolk Genealogy 16,* pp. 53-56.

Norfolk continued

Parishes in the detached deaneries of Heacham and Burnham (**H**), and Repps and Waxham (**R**), in the archdeaconry of Norfolk and in the detached deaneries of Breccles (**B**) and Thetford (**T**) in the archdeaconry of Norwich; parishes in the peculiars of the Dean and Chapter of Norwich (**DC**), Castle Rising (**CR**), and Great Cressingham (**GC**); and the parish of Emneth in the diocese of Ely (**E**).

Aldborough **R**; Antingham **R**; Arminghall **DC7**; Ashill **B**; Ashmanhaugh **R**; Aylmerton **R**; Bacton **R**; Bagthorpe **H**; Barmer **H**; Barningham Norwood **R**; Barningham Town **R**; East, North and West Barsham, **H**; Barton Turf **R**; Barwick **H**; West Beckham **DC1**; Beeston Regis and St. Lawrence **R**; Bessingham **R**; Gt and Newton Bircham **H**; Bircham Tofts **H**; Bradfield **R**; Brancaster **H**; Breckles **B**; Brumstead **R**; Burnham Deepdale, Norton, Overy, Thorpe, Ulpe and Westgate **H**; Carbrooke **B**; Castle Rising **CR4**; Caston **B**; Catfield **R**; Catton **DC6**;North and South Creake **H**; Gt. Cressingham **GC8**; Cromer **R**; Crostwight **R**; Dilham **R**; Docking **H**; Dunton **H**; Eaton **DC7**; Eccles **R**; Edingthorpe **R**; Little Ellingham **B**; Emneth **E9**; Fakenham **H**; Felbridge **R**; Felmingham **R**; Fring **H**; Fulmodeston cum Croxton **H**; Gatesend **H**; Gimingham **R**; Gresham **R**; Griston **R**; Gunton **R**; Hanworth **R**;

Happisburgh **R**; Heacham **H**; Hempstead **R**; Hickling **R**; Hindolveston **DC3**; Holme next the Sea **H**; Honing **R**; Horning **R**; Horsey **R**; Houghton (next Harpley) **H**; Hoveton St. John and St. Peter **R**; Hunstanton **H**; Ingham **R**; Ingoldisthorpe **H**; Irstead **R**; Kettlestone **H**; Knapton **R**; Lakenham **DC7**; Lessingham **R**; Ludham **R**; Martham **DC5**; Matlask **R**; Merton **B**; Metton **R**; Mundesley **R**; Neatishead **R**; Northrepps **R**; **Norwich** (Cathedral, St. Helen, St. James, St. Paul) **DC7**; Overstrand **R**; Ovington **B**; Palling **R**; Paston **R**; Plumstead **DC6**; Potter Heigham **R**; Ridlington **R**; Ringstead **H**; Roughton **R**; Roydon near Lynn **CR4**; East and West Rudham **H**; Runton **R**; East Ruston **R**; Little Ryburgh **H**; Saham Toney **B**; Sco Ruston **R**; Scoulton **B**; Sculthorpe **H**; Sedgeford **DC2**; Sheringham **R**; Shernborne **H**; Sidestrand **R**; Sloley **R**; Smallburgh **R**; Snettisham **H**; Little Snoring **H**; Southrepps **R**; Sprowston **DC6**; Stalham **R**; Stanhoe **H**; Stibbard **H**; Stow Bedon **B**; Suffield **R**; Sustead **R**; Sutton **R**; Swafield **R**; Syderstone **H**; Tatterford **H**; Tattersett **H**; Thetford **T**; Thompson **B**; Thornham **H**; Thorpe Market **R**; Threxton **B**; Thurgarton **R**; Titchwell **H**; Tottington **B**; Triningham **R**; Trowse Newton **DC7**; Trunch **R**; Tunstead **R**; Walcott **R**; North Walsham **R**; Waterden **H**; Watton **B**; Waxham **R**; Westwick **R**; Witton (near North Walsham) **R**; North and South Wootton **CR4**; Worstead **R**.

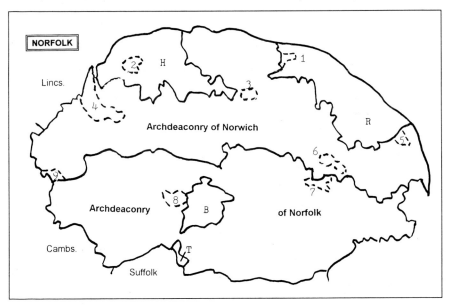

NORTHAMPTONSHIRE and RUTLAND

(Soke of Peterborough now in Cambridgeshire; Rutland now in Leicestershire.)

Since 1858: Probate Records for England and Wales are at the *Principal Registry of the Family Division, Somerset House, Strand, London WC2R 1LP.* Indexes to these to 1928 or later are held locally at the *Birmingham Reference Library; County Record Office, Huntingdon; Leicestershire Record Office;* and the *Bodleian Library, Oxford;* for other copies, see page 11.

Wills proved at Northampton, 1858-1930 (card index to 1880; in annual volumes 1881-1908) and Peterborough, 1858-1941 (indexed) are held locally at *Northamptonshire Record Office.* Original wills proved at Northampton, 1858-1930, are at *Birmingham District Probate Registry, Cavendish House, Waterloo Street, Birmingham B2 5PS.*

Peculiar of Banbury (Oxon), **7**
Kings Sutton (Northants); Grimsbury (Northants) (parish of Banbury)

Peculiar of Empingham (Rutland), **1**
Empingham, Hardwick

Peculiar of Gretton (Northants)
Duddington (**3**), Gretton (**5**)

Peculiar of Ketton (Rutland), **2**
Ketton, Geeston, Tixover

Peculiar of Liddington (Rutland), **4**
Liddington; Caldecott; Thorpe by Water (parish of Seaton).

Peculiar of Nassington (Northants), **6**
Nassington, Apethorpe, Woodnewton, Yarwell.

Before 1858: Northamptonshire and Rutland were in the province of Canterbury and diocese of Peterborough.

Apart from P.C.C. (see page 12), probate records for virtually the whole of both counties are at the

> **Northamptonshire Record Office,** *Northampton*

which issues a leaflet listing the various series of probate records there.

Since the 1590s the major, southern, part of Northamptonshire has been in the jurisdiction of the **Archdeaconry Court of Northampton**; the remainder of the county, the Soke of Peterborough and Rutland, were in the jurisdiction of the **Consistory Court of Peterborough**.

Before 1598 both courts had concurrent jurisdiction, so records from places in either area may be found in either court; but the bulk were always in the Northampton Archdeaconry Court. Records of both courts are at the *Northants. R.O.*

There is a published index to wills in the **Northampton Archdeaconry Court, 1510-1652,** *BRS 1*; MS index by H.I. Longden **1652-75**, and a card index **1676-1857.**

Calendars (with indexes) have been published to admons, **1545-46, 1638-41, 1660-1676** (by H.I. Longden); **1677-1710** *(BRS 70)*, **1711-1800** *(BRS 92;* Banbury Hist Soc **17**). MS calendars, by year, by H.I. Longden, **1801-1820** and original calendars, **1821-1857.**

Invs, **1660-1800,** are listed in the *BRS* vols, but there are many more, **1660-1670,** in the MS calendars, which were omitted from Longden's published volume. Visitors to the *Northants R.O.* should consult staff on which indexes to use.

There are no published indexes to the **Consistory Court of Peterborough** records. Wills: MS index (by H.I. Longden) **1541-1646** (gaps 1576-84, 1592-97), TS index **1604-1719** (also at *SofG*). Admons: TS index **1598-1684** (in original act books). Act books **1682-1719** relate both to wills and admons, with original indexes. Wills and admons, **1719-1857** (card index).

Exceptions:

Lincolnshire Archives Office holds probate records for several peculiars in both Northamptonshire and Rutland, most of which are indexed in *BRS 57.* There are microfilms of the documents at the *Northants R.O.*

The peculiars were, in Northamptonshire: **Gretton with Duddington 1657-1832** *(BRS 57);* **Nassington 1654-1753** *(BRS 57);* **1746-1844** (MS list); in Rutland: **Empingham 1669-1744** *(BRS 57),* **1745-1835** (MS list); **Ketton with Liddington 1666-1677** *(BRS 57)* (and see below).

Places in peculiars also occur in the records of the **Peculiar of the Dean and Chapter of Lincoln, 1534-1834** *(BRS 57).*

Records of the Rutland peculiars of **Caldecott, 1669-1820,** and **Ketton and Liddington, 1722-1820,** are at the **Leicestershire Record Office,** printed index in BRS *51*; and a few later records on card index.

The Northamptonshire parish of Kings Sutton, and Grimsbury, in the parish of Banbury, were in the **Peculiar of Banbury** with records at *Oxfordshire Archives,* fully indexed, **1547-1856,** in *Oxon Record Soc 40* and *Banbury Hist Soc 1*; Grimsbury will and inv abstracts **1591-1650** in *Banbury Hist Soc 13, 14.*

NORTHUMBERLAND

(Newcastle upon Tyne now in Tyne and Wear)

Since 1858: Probate Records for England and Wales are at the *Principal Registry of the Family Division, Somerset House, Strand, London WC2R 1LP.* The nearest locally held indexes are at *York Sub-Registry* (see page 11). For copies of the printed indexes held elsewhere, see page 11.

Registered copy wills proved at Newcastle, 1858-1941 (from 1926 also incl. Gateshead and places immediately south of the River Tyne) are deposited at the *Northumberland Record Office.* Originals, 1858-date, are at the *Newcastle District Probate Registry, Plummer House, Croft Street, Newcastle upon Tyne NE1 6NP.*

Before 1858: see with Co. Durham, page 25.

NOTTINGHAMSHIRE

Since 1858: Probate Records for England and Wales are at the *Principal Registry of the Family Division, Somerset House, Strand, London WC2R 1LP.* Indexes to these (to 1928) are held locally at *Nottinghamshire Archives.* For other copies, see page 11.

Registered copy wills to 1939 proved at Nottingham (to 1926 for Notts. only), indexed to 1935, are held locally at *Nottinghamshire Archives.*

Before 1858: Nottinghamshire was in the province and diocese of York. The county lay entirely (peculiars excepted) in the archdeaconry of Nottingham.

The original records of the archdeaconry and of the peculiars are now at

Nottinghamshire Archives, Nottingham.

There is a card index to all probate records for the **Archdeaconry of Nottingham** for the whole period from c.**1500-1857.**

There is also a separate card index to all probate records for the various **Peculiars,** including the important **Peculiar of Southwell,** from **1506** for the whole period.

Only the original wills of the archdeaconry are at Nottingham, many of which have not survived. There should usually be a registered copy at the

Borthwick Institute, York.

bound in with all the other exchequer and prerogative copy wills, within the period **1389-1857,** whilst those at Nottingham do not represent a complete set.

Nottinghamshire wills are also to be found in the **Prerogative Court of York,** at the Borthwick Institute. There are printed indexes to wills and admons for both **Prerogative** and **Exchequer Courts of York** (which include the Nottingham archdeaconry), indexed jointly, **1389-1688** *(Yorks. Arch. Soc. Record Series, 6, 11, 14, 19, 22, 24, 26, 28, 32, 35, 49, 60, 68, 89).* There is also a printed index to Notts wills and admons only (extracted from these volumes), **1568-1619.**

For **1688-1731** there is a TS index available at the *Borthwick Institute* (where the records are) and at *Nottinghamshire Archives.* There is a MS 19th century calendar to records after **1731,** to **1857.**

There are also a few records for the **Peculiars of Apesthorpe** or Habblesthorpe **(1577-1844)** and **Bole (1546-1847)** (TS indexes) at the *Borthwick Institute.*

Nottinghamshire testators are also to be found in the records of P.C.C. (see page 12), although, being in the province of York, these are far fewer than for counties in the southern province. *Nottinghamshire Archives* has a copy of the printed index to P.C.C., **1853-1857.**

For a map and full list, see page 42.

Nottinghamshire continued

Places in Nottinghamshire in jurisdictions other than the archdeaconry of Nottingham, though they are nevertheless also likely to be found in the exchequer (archdeaconry) records too.

A: Prebend of Apesthorpe;
B: Prebend of Bole;
E: Manor of Edwinstowe;
G: Manor of Gringley-on-the-Hill;
J: Manor of St. John of Jerusalem or Shelford St. Johns;
K: Peculiar of Kinoulton;
M: Manor of Mansfield;
R: Manor of Rufford Abbey;
S: Peculiar of Southwell;
T: Manor of Skegby and Teversal;
Y: Peculiar of the Dean and Chapter of York.

Note. The manorial court of St. John of Jerusalem (J) had jurisdiction, over the tenants of the manor only, in a number of places in the south of the county - these are not marked on the map.

Apesthorpe **A6**; Askham **Y**; Aslockton **J**; Barnby-in-the-Willows **J**; Beckingham **S&G4**; Bleasby **S**; Blidworth **S**; Bole **B**; Budby **M10**; Calverton **S**; Carburton **E**; Car Colston **J**; Carlton in Gedling **J**; Carlton on Trent **S11**; Caunton **S11**; Cotgrave **J**; Cropwell Bishop **S12**; Darlton **S9**; East Drayton **Y**; Dunham **S9**; Eaton **S7**; Edingley **S**; Edwinstowe **E**; Farnsfield **S**; Flintham **J**; Gedling **J**; Gringley-on-the-Hill **G2**; Halam **S**; Halloughton **S**; Hickling **J**; Holme **S11**; Hoveringham **J**; Hucknall under Huthwaite **M**; Kilton (Worksop) **M**; Kinoulton **K**; Kirklington **S**; Kneeton **J**; Laneham **Y**; North Leverton **S6**; Mansfield **M**; Mansfield Woodhouse **M**; Misterton **G&Y1**; Morton **S**; North and South Muskham **S11**; Normanton-on-Soar **J**; Normanton-on-the-Wolds **J**; Norwell **S11**; Owthorpe **J**; Oxton **S**; Plumtree **J**; Radcliffe-on-Trent **J**; Ragnall **S9**; Rampton **S8**; Rempstone **J**; Ruddington **J**; Rufford **R**; Scarrington **J**; Scofton (Worksop) **M**; Skegby **T**; Southwell **S**; Stanford-on-Soar **J**; West Stockwith **G&Y1**; Stokeham **Y**; Sutton-in-Ashfield **M**; Teversal **T**; Tollerton **J**; Upton **S**; Walkeringham **G3**; Warsop **M**; South Wheatley **S5**; Willoughby-on-the-Wolds **J**; Woodborough **S**; Worksop **M**.

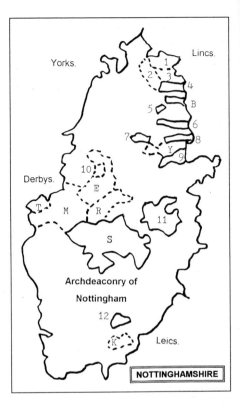

Yorks.

Lincs.

Derbys.

Archdeaconry of
Nottingham

Leics.

NOTTINGHAMSHIRE

OXFORDSHIRE

Since 1858: Probate records for England and Wales are at the *Principal Registry of the Family Division, Somerset House, Strand, London WC2R 1LP.* Indexes to these are held locally at the *Bodleian Library, Oxford (Radcliffe Camera, Lower Reading Room; charge for access),* and on microfiche, to 1935, at the *Centre for Oxfordshire Studies, Oxford Central Library.* For other copies, see page 11.

Before 1858: Oxfordshire was in the province of Canterbury and formed the diocese and archdeaconry of Oxford.

Apart from P.C.C. (see p. 12, and right), probate records for virtually the whole county are held at the

Oxfordshire Archives, *Oxford* (appointment necessary).

The probate records at *Oxfordshire Archives* comprise:

1. **Consistory and Archdeaconry Courts of Oxford,** covering the whole county except for peculiars. Consolidated index to all probate records, **1516-1732** (published *BRS 93, 94*); **1732-1857** (for publication by *BRS, 109,* 1997). Invs **1550-1590** printed in *Oxon Record Soc 44,* from Oxford consistory, archdeaconry and peculiar courts.

2. **Oxfordshire Peculiars** - the areas round Banbury in the north and Dorchester and Thame in the south - which are included, **1547-1856,** in the index in *BRS 109.* The only exception is Newington, in the **Peculiar of Monks Risborough,** whose records, **1605-1856,** are now at *Bucks R.O.,* page 17.

There is also a printed index to probate records of the **Peculiar of Banbury and Cropredy, 1547-1857,** and the **Manorial Court of Sibford Gower, 1733-1829** *(Oxon Record Soc 40* and *Banbury Hist Soc 1);* and abstracts of wills, admons and invs for Banbury itself, **1591-1650,** are printed in *Banbury H.S. 13* and *14.* Mid-16th century records for the peculiars are also found in the consistory and archdeaconry court records.

In addition, the

Bodleian Library, *Oxford*

houses the records of the **Court of the Chancellor of the University of Oxford.** These records are not administered by the Bodleian Library, and application to see them must be made to the *Deputy Keeper of the University Archives, c/o Bodleian.* Jurisdiction was restricted to resident members of the University, but others having connections with the University may appear in the records. There is a printed index to the complete period, wills and admons **1436-1814,** invs **1443-1740** *(An Index to Wills Proved in the Court of the Chancellor,* 1862).

M'film of abstracts of all probate material from this Court is at the *Society of Genealogists.*

Oxfordshire Testators in P.C.C.

Wills, **1393-1510,** are printed in full in *Oxon Record Soc 39.*

Printed indexes: full *BRS* (and others) series to **1700** on open shelves in *Selden End, Dept. of Western MSS, Bodleian Library.* Full index to England and Wales, **1853-1858,** on open shelves in *Radcliffe Camera, Lower Reading Room, Bodleian Library* (and microfiche edition at *Centre for Oxfordshire Studies).* Printed indexes to Oxfordshire testators in P.C.C., **1750-1800,** A-Sh only, in *Oxon FH 1, 6,* pp. 166-168, *3, 6* pp. 192-5, *4, 9* pp. 286-90, *6, 3* pp. 165-70 (from published index); and to all Oxon and Berks testators for year **1801,** *Oxon FH, I, 8,* pp. 216-20. Invs 1661-early C18, listed by parish in *Oxon Local History I, 2 & 3* (1981).

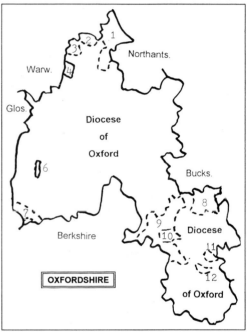

Places in Oxfordshire outside the jurisdiction of the consistory and archdeaconry courts of Oxford:

B : Peculiar of Banbury and Cropredy
M : Peculiar of Monks Risborough

Banbury **B1**; Benson (Bensington) **9**; Britwell Prior **9**; Chiselhampton **9**; Clifton Hampden **9**; Claydon **B1**; Cropredy **B1**; Dorchester **9**; Drayton St. Leonard **9**; Horley **B2**; Hornton **B2**; Langford **7**; Marsh Baldon **9**; Gt. Milton **9**; Mollington **B1**; Nettlebed **12**; Newington **M10**; Pishill **11**; Shenington (Glos., see page 27) **3**; Sibford (parish of Swalcliffe) **4**; Stadhampton **9**; Sydenham **8**; Tetsworth **8**; Thame **8**; Toot Baldon **9**; Warborough **9**; Wardington **B1**; Widford (Glos.) **6**.

RUTLAND
(now in Leicestershire)

Since 1858: Rutland was in the Leicester probate district and (in addition to the Principal Registry, page 11) registered copy wills proved at Leicester, **1858-1940** are deposited at the *Leicestershire Record Office* (card index to 1918). Original wills, **1858-1969**, are still at *Leicester Probate Registry* (page 34).

Before 1858: see with Northamptonshire, pages 40-41.

SHROPSHIRE

Since 1858: Probate records for England and Wales are at the *Principal Registry of the Family Division, Somerset House, Strand, London WC2R 1LP.* Indexes to these (to 1928) are held locally at the *Cheshire Record Office* and at the *Birmingham Reference Library;* for other copies, see page 11.

Registered copy wills proved at Shrewsbury (for Shropshire), 1858-1940, are deposited at *Shropshire Records and Research Centre*, indexed on m'fiche 1858-1940. Original wills 1930-42 are at the *Chester Probate Sub-Registry, Chester,* earlier wills are at the *P.R.O., Hayes.*

Places in Shropshire outside the jurisdictions of the consistory courts of Lichfield and Hereford.

Diocese of St. Asaph
Kinnerley, Knockin, Llanblodwel, Llanmynech, Melverley, Oswestry, St. Martins, Selattyn, Whittington.

Royal Free Chapel of Shrewsbury St. Mary
Albrighton (**5**); Astley (**6**); Clive (**4**); Shrewsbury St. Mary (**7**)

Peculiar of Longdon on Tern (8)

Peculiar of Wombridge Abbey (9)

Peculiar of Ashford Carbonell (12)

Peculiar Deanery of Bridgnorth
Bridgnorth (**10**); Alveley (**11**); Bobbington (**11**); Claverley (**11**); Quatford (**10**).

Manor of Ellesmere (1)
Ellesmere, Colemeare, Lyneal, Welshampton

Peculiar of Prees
Calverhall (**3**); Darliston (**3**); Prees (**3**); Whixall (**2**)

Diocese of Worcester
Halesowen (Salop, detached).

Shropshire continued

Before 1858: Shropshire was in the province of Canterbury, the south-western half lying in the diocese of Hereford and the north-eastern in the diocese of Lichfield (and Coventry); with a few extreme north-western parishes in the diocese of St. Asaph; and Halesowen in the diocese of Worcester. There were also several peculiars.

The location of the probate records in diocesan record offices reflect this division, most being at *Lichfield* or *Hereford*, and some at the *National Library of Wales, Aberystwyth.* For P.C.C. see page 12.

Lichfield Joint Record Office, Lichfield.

Consistory Court of Lichfield, wills and admons, **1516-1857**, 19th century MS calendar; a less accurate version of this to **1652** is printed in *BRS 7*. See also the note under Staffordshire (page 48) on a recently completed computerised index

Peculiar of Prees or Pipe Major Wills **1697-1857**, included in consolidated 19th century MS calendar to most peculiars at Lichfield, and printed to **1652** in *BRS 7*.

Records of other Shropshire peculiars (transferred from the *National Library of Wales*) are

Bridgnorth, 1663-1857 (printed index, *Salop Archaeological & Natural History Soc. Transactions, 4th series, vol. 12. pt.1,* 1929).

Ellesmere, C17-1857 (index *SANHS Trs, vol. 12, pt.2 (XLV),* 1930).

Buildwas, Longdon-on-Tern, Shrewsbury St. Mary, Tyrley, Wombridge, C17-1857 (index, *SANHS Trs, vol. 46, pt.1* 1931).

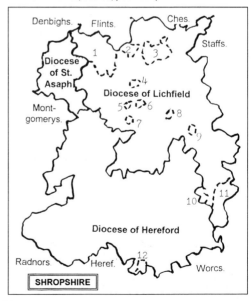

44

Shropshire continued

Record Office, Hereford.

Episcopal Consistory Court of Hereford (transferred from the *National Library of Wales*). Card index to wills **1600-1660**. Chronological list, wills and invs, **1539-1599**, invs **1628-1641**. After 1660, to 1857, indexes in act books to wills and admons.

Peculiar of Ashford Carbonell: Wills, admons, invs **1662-1857** (act book).

A consolidated index to all records in the Hereford consistory courts and peculiars is in preparation for publication by the *BRS*.

Records of nine parishes in north-western Shropshire in the diocese of **St. Asaph** are at the *National Library of Wales, Aberystwyth*, see pages 64-65.

Shropshire County Library, Shrewsbury, has wills and invs, **1665-1816** for the **Manor of Ruyton-of-the-Eleven-Towns**. Printed index to wills **1665-1709** (64 only) in *Salop. Arch. Soc. Trans., vol. 52*, pp. 116-18. Remainder unindexed.

See also *A List of Wills and Marriage Settlements in the Local History Collection of the Shrewsbury Public Library*, 1958 (mainly probate copies).

Halesowen, formerly a detached part of Shropshire, was in the jurisdiction of the **Consistory Court of Worcester**, at *Worcester Record Office*, printed indexes to **1652** *(BRS 31, 39)*, TS index **1660-1857**.

Prerogative Court of Canterbury (see also page 12). Printed index to **Shropshire wills 1700-1749** in *Shropshire Probates* by G.F. Matthews, 1929; and **1750-1770**, MS at *SofG*.

SOMERSET

(the northern part of the county is now in the county of Avon)

Since 1858: Probate records for England and Wales are at the *Principal Registry of the Family Division, Somerset House, Strand, London WC2R 1LP*. Indexes to these are held locally at the *Bristol Record Office* (1858-1900) and at Exeter (at *Exeter Probate Sub-Registry, Exeter*, see page 22). For other copies, see page 11.

Before 1858: Somerset was in the province of Canterbury and diocese of Bath and Wells.

For records of **P.C.C.**, see page 12; also printed abstracts of Somerset wills in **P.C.C.**, **1383-1558** *(Somerset Record Soc., vols. 16, 19, 21)*.

Somerset continued

All probate records for the diocese of Bath and Wells deposited in the probate registry at Exeter were destroyed by enemy action in 1942, so there are very few original records for the county apart from those in P.C.C. However over 15,000 copies have been located in more than 320 sources by Sir Mervyn Medlycott, and these are listed in *Somerset Wills Index: Printed and Manuscript Copies*, 1993, available as a book, £25 + p&p, or on microfiche, £4 + p&p, from Harry Galloway Publishing, 9 Drysdale Close, Milton, Weston-super-Mare, Som. BS22 8HH.

There are printed indexes to the lost wills and admons for the **Archdeaconry of Taunton, 1537-1799** *(BRS 45, 53)* and **Peculiar of Ilminster, 1690-1857** *(BRS 53)*; and to lost wills, **1528-1600**, in *Somerset R.S.*, vol. *62*, to the following jurisdictions: **Episcopal Consistory Court of Bath and Wells; Consistory Courts of: the Archdeaconry of Wells; the Dean of Wells;** and **the Dean and Chapter of Wells**.

There are MS indexes to the destroyed records at *SofG*, Episcopal Consistory to 1829; Archdeaconry of Wells, to 1799; Dean of Wells, to 1804, Dean and Chapter of Wells, wills to 1720, 1837-1857, admons, 1660-1857; Peculiars (individually) c1660-1857 (now available on m'fiche).

Somerset Archive and Record Service, *Taunton*
---

has **Death Duty Office** copies of most wills for the county from 1812 (for local courts and P.C.C.), card indexed. Also a MS collection of 32 vols. by F.A. Crisp, of P.C.C. and local court abstracts (partially printed in 6 vols., *Abstracts of Somerset Wills...*). These and other 'stray' wills are listed in the *Somerset Wills Index*.

Wills and admons **1805-1811** should be found amongst the **Death Duty Registers** abstracts at the *Public Record Office* (see page 14). Microfilms of these registers are held by the *Somerset R.O.*

Exception:
The Somerset parish of Abbots Leigh was in the jurisdiction of the **Consistory Court of Bristol**, records at the Bristol Record Office, page 27.

Other printed sources:
Somerset Parishes: a handbook of historical reference to all places in the county, by A.L. Humphreys, 1905, indexes many wills by parish.
Wills of Wellington and West Buckland 1372-1811, A.L. Humphreys, 1908.
The Municipal Records of Bath, 1189-1604, A.J. King and B.H. Watts, Appx.A, Part II.
Abstracts of wills, 1530-1599 (225) for Chew Magna, Chew Stoke, Dundry and Stowey in *Somerset Record Soc., vol. 62*.
Index to Somerset Wills and Admons, 1805-1857 (Estate Duty Office copies), David T. Hawkings;
Index to Somerset Probate Inventories (Somerset R.O. and P.R.O.), Adrian J. Webb.

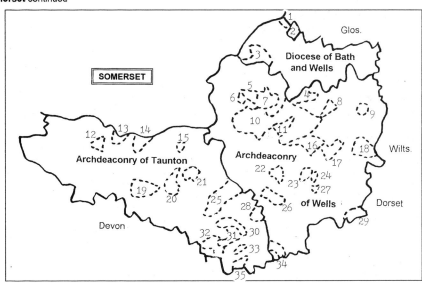

Somerset parishes outside archdeaconry jurisdiction:

B: Consistory court of Bristol,
C: Consistory court of the Dean and Chapter of Wells;
D: Consistory court of the Dean of Wells; **I:** Royal peculiar court of Ilminster;
P: other Wells peculiar and prebendal courts.

Abbots Leigh **B2**; (Chapel) Allerton **D10**; Ashill **P30**; South Barrow **C27**; Biddisham **D6**; Binegar **D8**; Bishops Lydeard **C20**; Broomfield **D21**; Buckland Dinham **P9**; Carhampton **D13**; Cheddar **C7**; Chesterblade **D17**; Chilcompton **D8**; Combe St. Nicholas **C32**; Compton Bishop **P5**; Compton Dundon **P22**; Cudworth **P33**; North Curry **C25**; St. Decumans **P14**; Dinder **D10**; Easton in Gordano **P1**; Evercreech **D17**; Fitzhead (pec. of Wiveliscombe) **P19**; East Harptree **P4**; Haselbury Plucknett **P34**; West Hatch **C25**; Henstridge **P29**; Ilminster **I-31**; Ilton **P30**; Kenn (pec. of Yatton) **P3**; Kingsbury Episcopi **P28**; Knowle (pec. of Cudworth) **P33**; East Lambrook (pec. of Kingsbury) **P28**; Litton **P4**; Lovington **C24**; Bishops Lydeard C20; West Lydford **P23**; Mark **D10**; Pilton **P16**; Priddy **D10**; St. Decumans **P14**; Stoke St. Gregory **C25**; Nether Stowey **D15**; Long Sutton **C26**; Timberscombe **P12**; Wedmore **D10**; Wells (St. Cuthbert) **D10**; (Liberty of St. Andrews) **C10**; Westbury **D10**; Whitelackington **P30**; Winsham **C35**; Witham Friary **P18**; Wiveliscombe **P19**; Wookey **P11**; North Wootton **P16**; Yatton **P3**.

STAFFORDSHIRE and DERBYSHIRE

(the southern tip of Staffordshire, round Walsall, Wednesbury, West Bromwich and Wolverhampton, is now in the county of West Midlands.)

Since 1858: Probate records for England and Wales are at the *Principal Registry of the Family Division, Somerset House, Strand, London WC2R 1LP.* Indexes to these (to 1928) are held locally at the *Birmingham Reference Library* and at *Nottinghamshire Record Office;* for other copies, see page 11.

Registered copy wills proved at Lichfield (for Staffordshire) 1858-1928 are deposited at the *Lichfield Joint Record Office* (indexed); those proved at Derby (for Derbyshire) 1858-1928 are at the *Derbyshire Record Office, Matlock* (also indexed). Original wills proved at Lichfield (to 1928) are at the *Birmingham District Probate Registry, Cavendish House, Waterloo Street, Birmingham B2 5PS.*

Before 1858: Staffordshire and Derbyshire were in the diocese of Lichfield and province of Canterbury.

Apart from P.C.C. (see page 12), virtually all the probate records for both counties are at

Lichfield Joint Record Office, Lichfield.

The *Lichfield Joint Record Office* issues a *Handlist to the Diocesan Records* (2nd edn., 1978) summarising the testamentary records.

There are good 19th cent MS calendars to the **Consistory Court of Lichfield, 1516-1857**; and to the various **Peculiars** in the diocese (one consolidated index, **1536-1857**). There are less accurate versions, to 1652, printed in *BRS 7*.

continued on page 48

Staffordshire and Derbyshire, continued

Places in the jurisdiction of courts other than the consistory court of Lichfield. All places in peculiars are likely to appear also in the consistory court records, and some places not actually in peculiars may still nevertheless be found in records of peculiars.

Staffordshire
(places in area '**B**' unless otherwise shown, except Stafford St. Chad). Clent and Dudley were in the diocese of Worcester.

Acton Trussell; Adbaston **7**; Alrewas; Upper Arley **13**; Armitage; Baswich; Bednall; Bentley; Bilbrook; Bilston; Blithbury; Branstone **5**; Brewood; Bromley Regis; Broughton **7**; Brownhills; Burton on Trent **5**; Bushbury; Cannock; Charnes **7**; Chorlton **7**; Clent **14**; Codsall; Colwich; Compton in Tettenham; Congreve; Coppenhall; Cotes **7**; Drayton in Hales **6**; Dudley (Worcs) **11**; Dunston; Eccleshall **7**; Edingale **9**; Farewell; Fradley, Fradswell **8**; Gnosall **7**; Hammerwich; Handsacre; Harborne **12**; Haselour; Hatherton; Great Haywood; Hilton in Wolverhampton; Hints; Horninglow **5**; Kings Bromley; Kinvaston; Levedale; Lichfield; Longdon, Mavesyn Ridware; Norton Canes; Oaken; High Offley **7**; Ogley Hay; Packington; Pattingham; Pelsall; Penkridge; Perton; Pipe Ridware; Rodbaston; Rugeley; Saredon; Sedgley **10**; Shareshill; Shobnall **5**; Shugborough; Slindon **7**; Smethwick **12**; Stafford St. Chad; Streethay; Stretton in Burton **5**; Stretton in Penkridge; Sugnall **7**; Swinfen; Tettenhall; Tipton; Trescott; Tyrley **6**; Wall; Walton **7**; Water Eaton; Wednesfield; Weeford; The Wergs; Wetmore **5**; Whittington; Willenhall; Wolverhampton; Wrottesley; Wyrley; Yoxall.

Derbyshire
(places in area '**A**' unless otherwise shown).

Ashford; Bakewell; Baslow; Beeley; Biggin; Breaston **3**; Burbage; Buxton; Chapel-en-le-Frith; Chelmorton; Dale Abbey **2**; Long Eaton **3**; Fairfield; Hartington; Hope; Kniveton **1**; Longstone; Monyash; High Needham; Peak Forest; Risley **3**; Sandiacre **3**; Sawley **3**; Sheldon; Stapenhill **4**; Earl Sterndale; Taddington; Tideswell; Wilne; Winshall **3**; Winster; Wormhill.

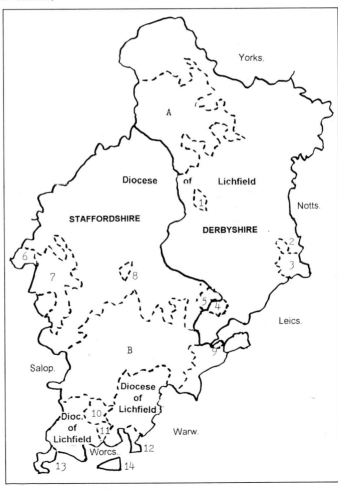

Staffordshire and Derbyshire, continued

Places in peculiars frequently also occur in the consistory court, so that index should always be consulted too.

There is a TS transcript and index of wills and admons in **Colwich Peculiar Court, 1614-1857**, copies at *Lichfield J.R.O.* and *SofG.*

Additional to these main indexes to the wills, admons etc, there is, at *Lichfield J.R.O.*, a recently compiled computerised index to cause papers, incl. accounts and invs from 1680 to 1850 (partial coverage only) (personal names: 32,071; places: 12,274 entries).

A **Staffordshire Probates Index** to records at *Lichfield J.R.O.* has been compiled by the *Birmngham and Midland Society for Genealogy and Heraldry.* This is alphabetical in time spans, mid 16th century to 1856, arranged by parish. Searches undertaken (state parish required, with donations to *B&MSGH* of £2 per surname per parish) by *Mr T. Bowers, 272 Walsall Road, Great Barr, Birmingham B42 1UB.*

Sheffield Archives has copies of wills and invs for Norton, Dore, Totley, Beighton, Mosbrough, formerly Derbys. but now in South Yorks.

Exceptions

Drayton-in-Hales, **Manor of Tyrley, 1695-1841**, records now at *Lichfield.*

Clent, Staffs, in the jurisdiction of the **Consistory Court of Worcester**, *Worcester Record Office*, see page 55.

Balterley, Staffs, in the jurisdiction of the **Consistory Court of Chester**, *Cheshire Record Office*, see page 19.

Peculiar of Dale Abbey, Derbys, records at *Nottinghamshire Record Office*, printed index **1753-1790** *(BRS 7)* and MS list, **1791-1857**.

Chesterfield wills and invs, **1521-1603**, are printed in *Derbys R.S. vol. 1*.

See also *Probate Inventories of* **Smethwick** *Residents, 1647-1747*, by Mary Bodfish, *Smethwick Local History Society, 1992.*

Places in **Suffolk** outside the jurisdiction of the archdeaconries of Suffolk and Sudbury:

Archdeaconry of Norfolk:
Rushford **(2)**

Archdeaconry of Norwich:
Thetford, Bramford,
Great Finborough **(1)**

Peculiar of Freckenham (3)

Peculiar of the Archbishop of Canterbury in the Deanery of Bocking:
Monks Eleigh **(5)**;
Hadleigh **(6)**;
Moulton **(4)**.

SUFFOLK

Since 1858: Probate records for England and Wales are at the *Principal Registry of the Family Division, Somerset House, Strand, London WC2R 1LP.* Indexes to these are held locally at the *Norwich Probate Sub-Registry, Norwich*, for other copies, see page 11. That formerly at Ipswich has been transferred to the *Sheffield Record Office.*

Registered copy wills proved at Bury St. Edmunds (West Suffolk district) 1858-1928 are now at the *Bury St. Edmunds branch* of the *Suffolk Record Office*. Those proved at Ipswich (East Suffolk and northern Essex) 1858-1941 are at the *Ipswich branch* of the *Suffolk Record Office,* and are indexed.

Before 1858: Suffolk was in the province of Canterbury and diocese of Norwich. The major collections of probate records are at the two branches of the *Suffolk Record Office: Ipswich* (Archdeaconry of Suffolk, covering East Suffolk); and *Bury St. Edmunds* (Archdeaconry of Sudbury covering West Suffolk). Suffolk testators are also to be found in the records of the consistory court of Norwich, at the *Norfolk Record Office*, as well, of course, as in P.C.C. - see page 12 and page 49, right.

The Suffolk R.O. publishes *A Guide to Genealogical Sources in Suffolk*, 4th edn., 1985, £6.50 + 70p p&p, which includes a very short section on probate records.

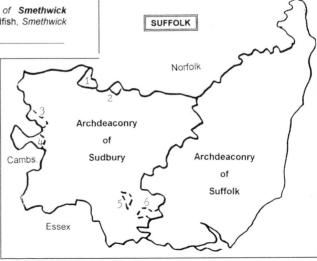

SUFFOLK

Norfolk

Archdeaconry
of
Sudbury

Archdeaconry
of
Suffolk

Cambs.

Essex

Suffolk, continued

Suffolk Record Office, Ipswich

has a free leaflet *Notes for Genealogists at Ipswich*. Published index *(BRS 90, 91)* to all probate records in the **Archdeaconry of Suffolk, 1444-1702,** superseding Crisp's Calendar, 1444-1600. The card index to later records, **1703-1857,** should if possible be used in preference to Gandy's Calendar, 1751-1793 (1929) which has been 'found wanting in many respects'. Published abstracts, 1620-24 *(Suffolk RS).* See also *Ipswich Probate Records (SRS 22).*

Printed abstracts: Wills **1620-1624** *(Suffolk Record Society 31,* 1989); Ipswich invs **1583-1681** *(Suffolk Record Society 22,* 1981).

Suffolk Record Office, Bury St. Edmunds

also issues a free leaflet on *Genealogical Sources.* The published index *(BRS 95, 96)* to all probate records in the **Archdeaconry of Sudbury, 1354-1700,** supersedes that to wills, 1354-1538, in *Proc. Suffolk Inst. Arch. 12.* MS index (on m'film), **1701-1799.** Card index, **1800-1857.** Printed abstracts of wills **1630-35** (894), **1636-38** *(SRS 29, 35).*

Also at this office are the records of the **Peculiar of Isleham** (Cambs) **and Freckenham** (Suffolk). Card index, wills **1556-1856,** admons, invs **1661-1817**; pre-1701 entries also in *BRS 95, 96.*

The *Lowestoft branch* of *Suffolk R.O.* also holds m'f of Archdeaconry of Suffolk wills, etc.

Norfolk Record Office, Norwich

has records of the **Consistory Court of Norwich.** As this court had superior jurisdiction throughout the diocese, Suffolk testators from throughout the county may be found here. There are printed indexes to wills **1370-1603** *(Norfolk Record Soc, 16,21; BRS 69, 73),* **1604-1857** *(Norfolk R.S. 28, 34, 38, 47).* For admons **1555-1857** see page 38.

Exceptions:

Rushford, in the **Archdeaconry of Norfolk,** see page 38.

Thetford, Bramford, Great Finborough, in the **Archdeaconry of Norwich,** page 38.

Monks Eleigh, Hadleigh, Moulton, in the **Peculiar** of the Archbishop of Canterbury in the **Deanery of Bocking,** at *Essex Record Office,* page 25. Wills **1627-1857** indexed in *BRS 79, 84.* Also TS abstracts, wills from **P.C.C.,** 1649-1660, admons **1665-83, 1722-38, 1756-1853** (at *SofG).*

Prerogative Court of Canterbury

There is a printed index to Suffolk wills in P.C.C, **1383-1604** *(Calendar* by T.W. Oswald-Hicks, 1913).

SURREY

Since 1858: Probate records for England and Wales are at the *Principal Registry of the Family Division, Somerset House, Strand, London WC2R 1LP;* see page 11.

Before 1858: Surrey was in the province of Canterbury and diocese of Winchester apart from the exempt deanery of Croydon, a peculiar of the archbishop of Canterbury. In 1845, the parishes which later constituted the Metropolitan area (Battersea, Bermondsey, Camberwell, Clapham, Lambeth, Newington, Rotherhithe, the Southwark parishes, Streatham, Tooting and Wandsworth) were transferred to the diocese of London.

See *Union Index of Surrey Probate Records which survive from before the year 1650,* Cliff Webb *(BRS 99).* This covers all courts including P.C.C. Apart from P.C.C. (see pages 12 and 50) most probate records for the county are at *London Metropolitan Archives.* Much, though not all, of this archive has been filmed by the Mormons and there are copies of the films at the *Surrey Local Studies Library, Guildford.*

The records at

London Metropolitan Archives (formerly G.L.R.O.)

comprise:

1. **Commissary Court of the Bishop of Winchester in the Archdeaconry of Surrey.** Wills and admons **1662-1751** (MS calendar); **1752-1857** (Index, *W. Surrey FHS 3,* 1983).

2. **Archdeaconry Court of Surrey.** Wills only. Index **1480-1650,** *BRS 99* as above; **1660-1751** (published); **1752-1857** (Index, *W. Surrey FHS 1,* 1981); abstracts **1480-90, 1595-1607** *(Surrey RS 4, 5,* 1915-21)).

3. **Consistory Court of London, 1514-1857.** From **1845** wills and admons from the Metropolitan area could be proved in this court (MS calendar).

Pre-Commonwealth records of Surrey testators are also to be found at the *Hampshire Record Office, Winchester,* in the **Consistory Court of Winchester,** indexed in *BRS 99* as above. A stray register of Surrey wills **1543-44** is in the *British Library* [Add. Ms. 24,925]. An indexed abstract is available at *London Metropolitan Archives., Surrey R.O.* and the *Society of Genealogists.*

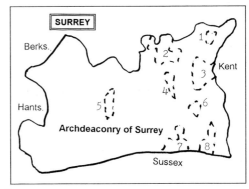

Surrey, continued

Lambeth Palace Library, *London*

has records of the **Peculiar of the Archbishop of Canterbury in the Deanery of Croydon,** including the Surrey parishes of Barnes (**2**), Burstow (**8**), Charlwood (**7**), Cheam (**4**), Croydon (**3**), East Horsley (**5**), Merstham (**6**), Mortlake (**2**), Church Newington (**1**), Putney (**2**), Roehampton (**2**), Walworth St. Peter (**1**) and Wimbledon (**2**).

Good MS index to all records, **1614-1821** (also TS copies at *P.R.O.* and *SofG*) and pre-1650 indexed in *BRS* **99** as above.

Prerogative Court of Canterbury

Pre-1650 probate records indexed in *BRS* **99** as above. Index to Surrey wills proved in **P.C.C. 1650-1700** (*West Surrey FHS* **9**, 1989). Printed abstracts, Surrey wills **1600-1610**, *Surrey Arch. Collns* **10-13, 23, 24**. Surrey *Admons. in PCC 1760-1781*, comp. A. Ridley, ed. C. Webb, WS FHS Record Series **17**.

Index to 6,000 Surrey invs C16-C19, all courts incl. P.C.C., pubd. *Domestic Building Research Group (Surrey)*, 1986.

SUSSEX

Since 1858: Probate records for England and Wales are at the *Principal Registry of the Family Division, Somerset House, Strand, London WC2R 1LP.* Indexes to these (to 1934) are held locally at the *East Sussex Record Office, Lewes,* and at the *Hampshire Record Office, Winchester;* for other copies, see page 11.

Registered copy wills proved at Chichester (for West Sussex) to 1928 are deposited at the *West Sussex Record Office, Chichester,* and are indexed.

Before 1858: Sussex was in the province of Canterbury and diocese of Chichester. The two archdeaconries of Chichester and Lewes corresponded approximately to the pre-1974 civil divisions of West and East Sussex. Their records are now respectively at the *West* and *East Sussex Record Offices.*

Sussex, continued

West Sussex Record Office, *Chichester.*

See *Genealogists' Guide to Sources in the W.S.R.O.,* P. Wilkinson, 1983.

Apart from P.C.C. (see page 12 and right) virtually all probate records for West Sussex are here, the majority in the Consistory Court of the Bishop of Chichester for the **Archdeaconry of Chichester.** There are printed indexes to wills **1479-1800** (*BRS* **49**) and admons **1555-1800** (*BRS* **64**) (see also *Sussex Notes and Queries* **12**, pp.37-39 for omitted admons **1675-1676**).

Card index, wills and admons **1801-57** and to other wills and admons C16-C18, omitted from printed indexes. Index to invs **1521-1834** pub. on microfiche (1981).

(Pre-1974) West Sussex parishes in the archdeaconry of Lewes:

Beeding, Crawley, Cowfold, Henfield, Kingston, Ifield, Shermanbury, Old and New Shoreham, Southwick, Woodmancote.

Sussex parishes outside the jurisdiction of the archdeaconries of Lewes and Chichester.

B : Deanery of Battle;
C : Peculiar of the Dean of Chichester;
M : Deanery of South Malling;
P : Deaneries of Pagham and Tarring;
R : Diocese of Rochester.

Battle **B5**; South Bersted **P9**; Buxted **M3**; Chichester All SS **P7**; Chichester (rest) **C7**; (The) Cliff **M3**; Durrington **P12**; Edburton **M13**; Fishbourne **C7**; Framfield **M3**; Glynde **M3**; Heene **P12**; Isfield **M3**; Lamberhurst **R2**; East Lavant **P6**; St. Thomas Lewes **M3**; Lindfield **M4**; South Malling **M3**; Mayfield **M3**; Pagham **P9**; Patching **P11**; Plaistow in Kirdford **P1**; Ringmer **M3**; Rumboldswyke **C7**; Slindon **P10**; Stanmer **M14**; Tangmere **P8**; West Tarring **P12**; Uckfield **M3**; Wadhurst **M3**.

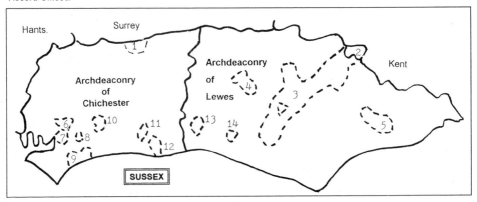

Sussex, continued

Also at the *West Sussex R.O.* are the records of the peculiar courts of:

1. **The Dean of Chichester** (jurisdiction over all Chichester parishes except All Saints; also Fishbourne and Rumboldswyke). Printed index, wills **1553-1643, 1660-1800**; admons **1577-1626, 1660-1768** *(BRS 64)*; card index to later wills and admons up to 1858 and to others omitted from the printed indexes.

2. **Deaneries of Pagham and Tarring** (for jurisdiction see list and map below). Printed index, wills **1516-1648**, admons **1560-1670** *(BRS 64)*; card index to later wills and admons up to 1858 and to others omitted from the printed indexes.

Most probate records for East Sussex (apart from P.C.C., see page 12) are at

East Sussex Record Office, *Lewes*

which issues a booklet *How to trace the History of your Family* summarising the testamentary records in the office; and also a free leaflet *Your County Record Office.*

The main holding is that of the Consistory Court of the Bishop of Chichester for the **Archdeaconry of Lewes.** This covers virtually the whole of East Sussex and also the (pre-1974) West Sussex parishes listed left. Printed index to wills and admons **1518-1652** *(BRS 24)* and TS index **1660-1857.**

Also at the *East Sussex R.O.* are records of two peculiars (for jurisdictions see list and map, left);

1. **Deanery of Battle.** Printed indexes, wills **1531-1617**, admons **1548, 1672-1617** *(BRS 24)*; wills and admons **1657-1856** *(Sussex Genealogist and Local Histn.*, vol. **1**, no. 1, June 1979).

2. **Deanery of South Malling.** Printed indexes: wills and admons **1559-1567** *(BRS 64; Sussex Arch. Soc. Colln, 50,* pp. 138-146) (these documents are at the *West Sussex R.O.* but microfilm of them is at the *East Sussex R.O.*); wills **1588-1646** *(BRS 24)*, card index (by M.J. Burchall), wills and admons **1559-1857** (see also *Sussex Family Historian* vol. **3**, no. 2, Sept 1977).

Exception

Lamberhurst (Kent and East Sussex) was partly in the jurisdiction of the Consistory and Archdeaconry Courts of Rochester, Kent, see page 32.

Sussex Testators in P.C.C.

There is a printed index to wills of Sussex testators apparently omitted from P.C.C. records, but now at *West Sussex R.O.* **1614-70** *(BRS 64)* and TS index.

See also *A Guide to Sussex Probate Records,* M.J. Burchall, 1981 - now somewhat out of date.

WARWICKSHIRE

(the north-west, Birmingham and Coventry area, is now in West Midlands)

Since 1858: Probate records for England and Wales are at the *Principal Registry of the Family Division, Somerset House, Strand, London WC2R 1LP.* Indexes to these (to 1928) are held locally at the *Birmingham Reference Library, Local Studies Department.* See also page 11.

Registered copy wills proved at Birmingham (for Warwickshire) to 1941 are also at the *Birmingham Reference Library* (not indexed). Original wills are at the *Birmingham District Probate Registry, Cavendish House, Waterloo Street, Birmingham B2 5PS.*

Before 1858: Warwickshire was in the province of Canterbury and split between the diocese of Lichfield and Worcester. As a result, the main collections of probate records are outside the county (and the modern county of West Midlands). For P.C.C. see page 12.

Records of the major, north-eastern, part of the county are at the

Lichfield Joint Record Office, *Lichfield*

which issues a *Handlist to the Diocesan Probate and Church Commissioners' Records* (2nd edn, 1978), summarising the testamentary records.

There is a good 19th century calendar to the **Consistory Court of Lichfield,** wills and admons, **1516-1857.** A separate index to records of **Peculiars** there includes the parishes of Arley, Bishops Itchington, Bishops Tachbrook, Edgbaston and Merevale, wills and admons **1536-1857** (one consolidated index). There are less accurate printed versions of these indexes to 1652 in *BRS 7.*

See also the entry under Staffordshire.

There is an Index to **Birmingham Probates** (incl. Aston, Handsworth, Edgbaston etc), **1500's** to **1857**, of records at *Lichfield J.R.O.* prepared by the *Birmingham & Midland SG&H.* Details as for the Staffordshire Probates Index, page 48.

Records of the south-western part of the county are mainly at the

Record Office, County Hall, *Worcester*

in the **Consistory Court of Worcester.** The 71 Warwickshire parishes in this diocese are listed on page 52. Printed indexes to wills **1451-1652,** admons **1520-1652** *(BRS 31, 39)*; TS index to wills, admons and invs, **1660-1857.**

The Shakespeare's Birthplace Trust, *Stratford-upon-Avon*

has records of two peculiars (for jurisdictions see list and map, page 52):

1. **Stratford upon Avon,** wills and admons, **1559, 1585-1634, 1653, 1658-1849** (TS index).

2. **Hampton Lucy,** wills, admons and invs, **1678-1795** (MS index).
See also the consistory court of Worcester.

Warwickshire, continued

Warwickshire Record Office, Warwick
---

holds records of the **Peculiars of Baddesley Clinton, Barston, Knowle, Packwood** and **Temple Balsall.** Printed index wills and admons **1675-1790** *(BRS 7).* MS calendar, post-1790 records; also Temple Balsall 1652-1741, copy at *Worcester Record Office.*

Exceptions

Welford and Weston-upon-Avon, in the jurisdiction of the **Consistory Court of Gloucester,** *Gloucestershire Record Office,* see page 27.

Mollington (partly Oxon) in parish of Cropredy (Oxon), in the jurisdiction of the **Peculiar of Banbury and Cropredy,** at *Oxfordshire Archives,* see page 43.

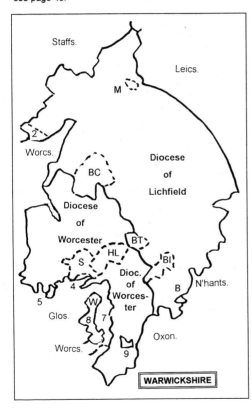

Warwickshire parishes in the diocese of **Worcester:**
Alcester, Gt. Alne, Alveston, Arrow, Aston Cantlow, Atherston on Stour, Barcheston, Barford, Barton on the Heath, Bearley, Beaudesert, Bidford, Billesley, Binton, Brailes, Budbrooke, Burmington, Butlers Marston, Charlecote, Cherington, Claverdon, Long Compton, Compton Verney, Compton Wynyates, Coughton, Eatington, Exhall, Halford, Hampton Lucy, Haseley, Haselor, Hatton, Henley in Arden, Honington, Idlicote, Ilmington (detd. **W8**), Ipsley, Kineton, Kinwarton, Lapworth, Lighthorne, Loxley, Moreton Morrell, Morton Bagot, Newbold Pacey, Norton Lindsey, Oxhill, Pillerton Hersey and Priors, Preston Bagot, Rowington, Salford, Sherbourne, Snitterfield, Spernall, Stratford-upon-Avon, Stretton on the Fosse (detd.**W8**), Studley, Tanworth, Temple Grafton, Tysoe, Ullenhall, Warwick, Wasperton, Weethley, Wellesbourne, Whatcote, Whichford, Whitchurch (detd **W8**), Wixford, Gt. Wolford, Wolverton, Wootton Wawen, Wroxhall.

Peculiar of Stratford upon Avon (S)
Stratford upon Avon, Bishopton, Bridgetown, Clopton, Dodwell, Drayton, Luddington, Shottery, Welcombe.

Peculiar of Hampton Lucy (HL)
Hampton Lucy, Alveston, Charlecote, Wasperton.

Places in these two peculiars also occur in the consistory court of Worcester.

Peculiar of Bishops Itchington (BI)
Bishops Itchington, Chadshunt, Gaydon.

Peculiar of Bishops Tachbrook (BT)

Peculiars of Baddesley Clinton, Barston, Knowle, Packwood and **Temple Balsall (BC)**

Peculiar of Merevale (M)

Peculiar of Banbury and Cropredy (B)
Mollington.

Peculiar of the Dean and Chapter of Lichfield
Edgbaston (2).

Diocese of Gloucester
(parishes partly in Glos.)
Welford (5), Weston upon Avon (4), Sutton-under-Brailes (9).

Diocese and County of Worcester (7)
(Worcs. parishes detached)
Alderminster, Shipston on Stour, Tidmington, Tredington.

WESTMORLAND
See with Cumberland, pages 20 and 21.

WILTSHIRE

Since 1858: Probate records for England and Wales are at the *Principal Registry of the Family Division, Somerset House, Strand, London WC2R 1LP.* Indexes to these are held locally at the *Hampshire Record Office, Winchester* (to 1935) and at the *Bristol Record Office* (to 1900). For other copies, see page 11.

Registered copy wills proved at Salisbury, 1858-1928, are at the *Wiltshire Record Office* and are indexed.

Before 1858: Wiltshire was in the province of Canterbury and diocese of Salisbury.

Apart from P.C.C. (see page 12 and below) virtually all probate records for the county are at the

---
Wiltshire Record Office, Trowbridge.

See *Sources for the History of a Wiltshire Family* (1981).

The county is mainly divided between the **Archdeaconries of Salisbury** (suthern Wiltshire) and **Wiltshire** (northern Wiltshire). There are, however, numerous parishes outside the jurisdiction of either archdeaconry. These were in the **Archdeaconry of the Sub-Dean of Salisbury** or in one of the many peculiars, and are listed on page 54. See also the **Consistory Court of Salisbury,** which at times had jurisdiction in all parishes in the county, and had sole jurisdiction in the Bishop's peculiars.

There are no published indexes or calendars. Those at the *Wiltshire R.O.* are 19th century MS calendars, with modern additions, to all probate records, individually to each court.

Archdeaconry of Salisbury: wills **1528-1857**; admons and invs **1540-1857.**

Archdeaconry of Wiltshire: wills **1557-1857**, admons and invs **1587-1857** (also TS index to 1799, copy at *SofG*).

Episcopal Consistory Court of Salisbury: wills **1526-1857**, admons and invs **1584-1857.**

Other courts in Wiltshire, outside the jurisdiction of the archdeaconries of Salisbury and Wiltshire:-

Archdeaconry of the Sub-Dean of Salisbury (jurisdiction: Salisbury except the Close, Milford, Stratford-sub-Castle): wills **1581-1588**, wills, admons and invs **1584, 1611-1857** (modern MS calendar).

Peculiars:

Dean of Salisbury (jurisdiction incl. Salisbury Close and eight parishes in Wilts, seven Berkshire parishes and 28 Dorset parishes or chapelries; also occasionally other parishes as shown in the list on page 54): wills, admons and invs **1557-1857** (19th cent MS calendar). See also 'Miscellaneous Wills' right

Dean and Chapter of Salisbury: 1600-1857.
Precentor of Salisbury: 1614-1857.
Prebend of Calne: 1610-1857

Dean and Canons of Windsor in Wantage: 1669-1840 (see also court of the Dean of Salisbury).

Castle Combe: 1669-1786 (thereafter see archdeaconry of Wiltshire).

Corsham: wills **1462-1857,** admons and invs **1720-1857** (19th century MS chronological list); wills **1662-1799,** admons and invs **1720-1799** (TS at SofG). See also archdeaconry of Wiltshire.

Savernake Forest: 1617-1829 (jurisdiction: Great and Little Bedwyn, see also Court of Dean of Salisbury and after 1829; Collingbourne Ducis, see also Consistory Court and after 1829).

For the following **prebendal peculiars** see also the court of the **Dean of Salisbury,** and 'Miscellaneous Wills' below:

Bishopstone: 1625-1799, 1800-1854.
Chute and Chisenbury: 1608-1799, 1800-1855.
Coombe and Harnham: 1648-1799, 1800-1855.
Durnford: 1634-1799, 1800-1857.
Highworth: 1609, 1623-1799, 1800-1857.
Hurstbourne and Burbage: 1635-1799, 1800-1856.
Netheravon: 1597-1799, 1800-1854.
Trowbridge: see Miscellaneous Wills.
Wilsford and Woodford: 1615-1854.

Miscellaneous Wills: many of these relate to the courts of the Dean and the Sub-Dean of Salisbury. Index: wills **1540-1809** (TS, superseding printed index of (Wilts.) wills **1540-1809** (*Wilts. Arch and Nat Hist Mag, vol. 45,* pp.36-67) but now incomplete).

Exceptions:

Kingswood and Marston Meysey were in the jurisdiction of the **Consistory Court of Gloucester,** page 27.

Whitsbury and West Wellow were in the jurisdiction of the **Consistory Court of Winchester,** see pages 28-29.

A computerised consolidated index to all **Wiltshire** wills (**1242-1887**) (based on existing MS indexes) is being prepared by *Dr Barbara J. Carter, 28 Oxus Road, Swindon, Wilts. SN1 4JQ* (send SAE for information and fees). At present this has about 30,000 out of an estimated 100,000 entries. It already includes all P.C.C. Wilts. entries, 1653-1660.

For a map of the county and list of parishes, see page 54.

Wiltshire, continued

Parishes in Wiltshire outside the jurisdiction of the archdeaconries of Salisbury and Wiltshire.

B : Prebend of Bishopstone; **C** : Prebend of Chute and Chisenbury; **CB** : Prebend of Combe (Bisset) and Harnham; **CC** : Peculiar of Castle Combe; **CG** : Consistory Court of Gloucester; **CS** : Consistory Court of Salisbury (in Bishop's Peculiars); **CW** : Consistory and Archdeaconry Courts of Winchester; **D** : Prebend of Durnford; **DC** : Peculiar Court of the Dean of and Chapter of Salisbury; **DS** : Peculiar Court of the Dean of Salisbury; **H** : Prebend of Highworth; **HB** : Prebend of Hurstbourne and Burbage; **N** : Prebend of Netheravon; **P** : Peculiar Court of the Precentor of Salisbury; **SD** : Archdeaconry of the Sub-Dean of Salisbury; **SF** : Peculiar of the Lord Warden of Savernake Forest; **T** : Peculiar of Trowbrige; **TC** : Peculiar Court of the Treasurer in the Prebend of Calne; **VC** : Peculiar of the Perpetual Vicar of Corsham; **W** : Peculiar of the Dean and Canons of Windsor in Wantage; **WW** : Prebend of Wilsford and Woodford.

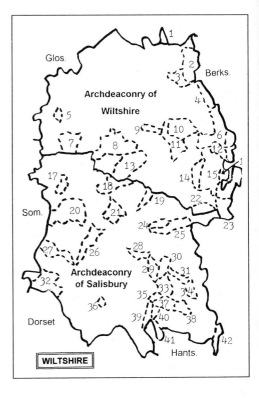

WILTSHIRE

Alderbury **TC38**; Baydon **DS6**; Gt. & Lit. Bedwyn **SF&DS15**; Berwick Bassett **TC9**; Berwick St. James **CS28**; Bishops Cannings **DC13**; Bishopstone **B&DS4**; Blackland (Calne) **TC8**; Bramshaw **DC42**; Bratton (Westbury) **P20**; Britford **DC37**; Broad Blunsdon **H&DS2**; South Broom **DC13**; Burbage **HB&DS14**; Calne **TC8**; Castle Combe **CC5**; Cherhill (Calne) **TC8**; Chisenbury **C&DS24**; Chute **C&DS23**; Collingbourne Ducis **SF&CS22**; Coombe Bissett **CB&DS39**; Corsham **VC&CS7**; (also archd. of Wilts); Devizes **CS18**; Dilton (Westbury) **P20**; Durnford **D&DS30**; Farley **TC34**; Figheldean **TC25**; (West) Harnham **CB&DS35**; Heytesbury **DS26**; Highworth **H&DS2**; Hill Deverill **DS27**; Homington **DC40**; Horningsham **DS27**; Hungerford **W&DS12**; Kingswood **CG** (detd); Lake (Wilsford) **WW&DS19**; West Lavington **CS21**; Marlborough **CS11**; Marston Meysey **CG1**; South Marston **H&DS2**; Mere **DS32**; Milford **SD&CS33**; Netheravon **N&DS24**; Ogbourne St. Andrew and St. George **W&DS10**; Pitton **TC34**; Potterne **CS18**; Preshute **CS11**; Ramsbury **DS6**; Salisbury **SD&CS33**; Salisbury Close **DS33**; Sevenhampton **H&DS2**; Shalbourne **W&DS16**; Southbroom **DC13**; Staverton (Trowbridge) **CS&T17**; Stert **CS18**; Stratford-sub-Castle **SD&CS33**; Stratton St. Margaret **VC&CS3** (also arch of Wilts); Swallowcliffe **DS36**; Trowbridge **CS&T17**; Tytherington (Heytesbury) **DS26**; West Wellow **CW42**; Westbury **P20**; Whitsbury or Whichbury **CW41**; Wilsford **WW&DS19**; Winterbourne Dauntsey **C&DS31**; Woodford **WW&DS29**.

WORCESTERSHIRE
(now part of Hereford and Worcester; northern tip in West Midlands county).

Since 1858: Probate records for England and Wales are at the *Principal Registry of the Family Division, Somerset House, Strand, London WC2R 1LP.* Indexes to these are held locally at the *Birmingham Reference Library;* see also page 11.
Registered copy wills proved at Worcester (for Worcestershire) 1858-1928 are deposited at the *Record Office, Worcester.* There is a duplicated TS index to these wills, copies at *SofG* and elsewhere. the original wills 1858-1928 are at the *Birmingham Probate Registry, Birmingham.*

Before 1858: Worcestershire was in the province of Canterbury and diocese of Worcester, apart from a few parishes in the diocese of Hereford and at times in Gloucester.
Apart from P.C.C. (see page 12) most probate records for the county are at the

> **Record Office (Hereford and Worcester C.C.),**
> *County Hall, Worcester.*

The office issues a leaflet on probate records in its custody. These comprise

1. Consistory Court of Worcester. By far the most important collection, covering the whole county (and diocese) apart from places listed right.
Printed indexes, wills **1451-1495, 1509-1652,** admons and invs **1520-1652** *(BRS 31, 39).* TS indexes, **1660-1857** (in four parts). TS index to a volume of copies of wills, incl. wills proved in London, during the Protectorate, **1652-1739.**

2. Dean and Chapter of Worcester, with jurisdiction over the following peculiars:
Berrow, 1670-1786;
Kempsey, 1668-1779;
Norton nr. Kempsey, 1668-1785;
Stoulton, 1668-1787;
Tibberton, 1770-1788;
St. Michael in Bedwardine and the College precincts, 1669-1783.
See also the Consistory Court.

3. Other peculiars:
Alvechurch or Allchurch, 1718-1773;
Bredon with Norton and Cutsdean, 1718-1773;
Fladbury (incl. Wyre Piddle, Throckmorton, Stock, Bradbury), 1642-1795;
Hanbury, 1720-1784 (and act book 1647-1762);
Hartlebury, 1720-1784;
Ripple with Queenhill and Holdfast, 1663-1727 (act book), 1721-1779;
Tredington, 1691-1697 (act book), 1717-1788.

Records of twenty Worcestershire parishes or chapelries (listed below) are at the

> **Record Office, Hereford**

in the jurisdiction of the **Episcopal Consistory Court of Hereford.** Card index to wills, **1600-1660.** Chronological list, wills and invs, **1539-1599,** invs **1628-1641.** Indexes in act books to wills and admons, **1660-1857.**

Worcestershire parishes, detached from the main county, or in peculiars, but still also in the jurisdiction of the **Consistory Court of Worcester;** and those in the jurisdiction of the Consistory Court of Hereford.

Detached parishes in the diocese of Worcester:
Alderminster **10**; Blockley **16**; Daylesford **19**; Dudley **1**; Evenlode **18**; Shipston on Stour **14**; Tidmington **14**.

Peculiars (also subject to the Consistory Court of Worcester):
Alvechurch **3**; Berrow **15**; Bradbury **9**; Bredon **13**; Bredons Norton **13**; Cutsdean **17**; Fladbury **9**; Hanbury **5**; Hartlebury **4**; Holdfast **12**; Kempsey **8**; Norton (nr. Bredon) **13**; Norton (nr. Kempsey) **8**; Queenhill **12**; Ripple **12**; Stock **9**; Stoulton **8**; Throckmorton **9**; Tibberton **6**; Tredington **11**; Wolverley **2**; Worcester, College Precincts and St. Michael in Bedwardine **7**; Wyre Piddle **9**.

Parishes and chapelries in the diocese of Hereford:
Abberley, Bayton, Bockleton, Clifton on Teme, Eastham, Edvin Loach, Hanley Child and William, Knighton-on-Teme, Kyre Magna and Parva, Lindridge, Mamble, Orleton, Pensax, Rock, Lower Sapey, Stanford-on-Teme, Tenbury.

WORCESTERSHIRE

Staffs. 1
Shropshire 2
Diocese of Hereford 4
Diocese of Worcester
Warwicks.
Heref.
Glos.

THE PROVINCE OF YORK

Before 1858: The Prerogative Court of York (P.C.Y.) had jurisdiction over the whole province: that is, in addition to the diocese of York itself, the dioceses of Carlisle, Chester, Durham and Sodor and Man. This jurisdiction was over any person having goods either in more than one jurisdiction within the diocese of York, or in more than one diocese in the northern province, or in both northern and southern provinces. Unless a person is known to have had widespread property it is best to search first the probate records of the diocese in which the deceased died.

At times, two other courts exercised the functions of P.C.Y. These were the **Chancery Court of the Archbishop of York** and the **Court of the Dean and Chapter of York.**

Records of these courts are all at

> **The Borthwick Institute of Historical Research,** York.

There are guides to *Genealogical Sources* (1981) and the *Archive Collections* (1973) and leaflets on the *Probate Records of the Diocese of York* and on *How to Find a Will.* See also Borthwick Institute Wallet **4**, *16th and 17th Century Wills, Inventories and Other Probate Documents.* Space is very limited and an appointment must be made in advance.

For the **Prerogative Court of York** there are printed indexes to wills and admons **1389-1688** *(Yorks Arch Soc Record Series **4, 6, 11, 14, 19, 22, 24, 26, 28, 32, 35, 49, 60, 68, 89**).* These indexes also include the Exchequer Court of York (see Yorkshire, right) and the **Court of the Dean and Chapter of York** (for which, **1321-1724**, see also *YAS **38**).* There is a TS index to P.C.Y. (only), **1688-1731**; and MS calendars (jointly with the Exchequer Court), **1731-1857.**

The Dean and Chapter had jurisdiction during archiepiscopal vacancies, but, except for the year 1724 (for which there is a contempory calendar), records are calendared with P.C.Y.

For the **Chancery Court of the Archbishop of York** there is a printed index to wills, admons and invs **1427-1658** (the earliest in fact Exchequer Court wills) (*Y.A.S.R.S.* **73**, erroneously entitled *Consistory Wills*), but since then a number of additional Chancery wills and invs have been found. See also wills in the archbishops' registers, **1316-1822** *(Y.A.S.R.S.* **93**);* **1825-1857** (*Borthwick Inst. Bulletin,* 1975, pp. 39-42).

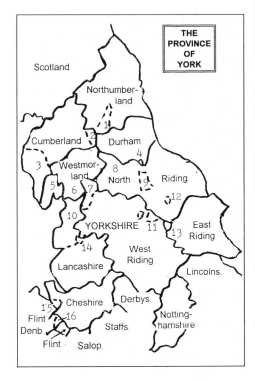

Apart from the areas listed below,

Cheshire was in the diocese of Chester;
Cumberland was in the diocese of Carlisle;
Durham was in the diocese of Durham;
Flintshire (southern detachment) was in the diocese of Chester;
Lancashire was in the diocese of Chester;
Northumberland was in the diocese of Durham;
Nottinghamshire was in the diocese of York;
Westmorland was in the diocese of Carlisle;
Yorkshire (all Ridings and the Ainsty of York [**13**]) was in the diocese of York;

In **Cumberland** the deanery of Copeland (**3**) was in the western division of the consistory court of the archdeaconry of Richmond (diocese of Chester), and the parish of Alston (**2**) was in the diocese of Durham.

In **Denbighshire** the parish of Holt (**16**) was in the diocese of Chester.

In **Flintshire** the peculiar of Hawarden (**15**) was in the diocese of Chester.

In **Lancashire** that part of the county north of the River Ribble (**5** and **10**) was in the western division of the consistory court of the archdeaconry of Richmond (diocese of Chester); and Aighton, Chaigley and Bailey (**14**) were in the diocese of York.

The Province of York, continued

In **Northumberland** the peculiar of Hexham and Hexhamshire (**1**) was in the jurisdiction of the archbishop of York until 1837; and Tockerington (Throckrington) (**1**) was a prebend of York.

In **Westmorland** the deaneries of Kendal and Lonsdale (**6**) were in the western division of the consistory court of the archdeaconry of Richmond (diocese of Chester).

In **Yorkshire, North Riding,** the deaneries of Richmond and Catterick (**8**) were in the eastern division of the consistory court of the archdeaconry of Richmond (diocese of Chester); the parish of Sockburn (**4**), the peculiar of Crayke (**12**) until 1837, and the bishop of Durham's peculiar of Allertonshire (**9**) until 1846 fell within the jurisdiction of the consistory court of Durham; and the parishes of Brompton, Deighton, High Worsall, Kirby Sigston; Northallerton and West Rounton (**9**) formed the peculiar of Allerton and Allertonshire under the jurisdiction of the dean and chapter of Durham until 1846.

In **Yorkshire, West Riding,** the deanery of Lonsdale (**7**) was in the western division of the archdeaconry of Richmond (diocese of Chester); the deanery of Boroughbridge (**11**) was in the eastern division.

Although **Lincolnshire** was in the Province of Canterbury, some Lincs. wills and admons appear in the records of P.C.Y. or of the Exchequer Court (right). An index to these is at the *Society of Genealogists* (see page 3).

YORKSHIRE

Since 1858: Probate records for England and Wales are at the *Principal Registry of the Family Division, Somerset House, Strand, London WC2R 1LP.* Indexes to these (to 1928) are held locally at the *West Yorkshire Record Office, Wakefield;* Sheffield Archives (prior notice required); and *York District Probate Registry, York.*

The county was long divided into the civil divisions of the North, East and West Ridings; and the city of York and the Ainsty (the area immediately surrounding the city); but these disappeared in the reorganisation of 1974.

Original wills proved at York since 1858 and at Wakefield (for the West Riding) 1858-1939 are at *York District Probate Sub-Registry.* Registered copy wills proved at Wakefield, 1858-1941, are at the *West Yorkshire County Record Office, Wakefield.*

Before 1858: Yorkshire was in the province of York (for P.C.Y. see left) and mainly in the diocese of York. The only major exception was the western half of the North Riding and a few parishes in the West Riding, which were in the eastern division of the archdeaconry of Richmond, part of the diocese of Chester.

Northern testators are relatively rare in **P.C.C.** (see page 12), except for the Interregnum, for which there is a printed index, wills and admons **1649-1660** *(Y.A.S.R.S. 1).* However, probates continued throughout this period in the Peculiar Courts of Masham and of the Forest of Knaresborough; and possibly in other Yorkshire courts.

Most probate records relating to the diocese, those of the Exchequer Court (the equivalent of a consistory court elsewhere), are now at

The Borthwick Institute, York (left).

The indexes to wills and admons are mainly in the same series as for P.C.Y. **1389-1688** *(Y.A.S.R.S.,* see left); **1688-1731** (separate TS); **1731-1857** (MS calendar with P.C.Y.).

For the **Chancery Court of York,** which also had jurisdiction in Yorkshire, see left.

Yorkshire, continued

The following parishes, chapelries and other places were at some or all of times outside the direct jurisdiction of the exchequer court of York. The civil division of the county into which each fell is shown by the initial letter in brackets following each name:

(A) = Ainsty of York; (E) = East Riding; (N) = North Riding; (W) = West Riding. Details of the exchequer court of York are given under 'Yorkshire' on page 57. Details of all other jurisdictions in the county are given under the Riding sections, and places may be located on the maps of each Riding. The peculiars of the dean and chapter, and of the dean, of York each covered a number of parishes; places in these and those subject to consistory or archdeaconry courts have the following keys:

AN = Archdeaconry of Nottingham (diocese of York); CC = Consistory of Chester; CD = Consistory of Durham; DC = Peculiar of the dean and chapter of York; DY = Peculiar of the dean of York; R = Archdeaconry of Richmond, eastern deaneries (diocese of York); RW = Archdeaconry of Richmond, western deaneries (diocese of Chester); SLH = Peculiar of St. Leonard's Hospital, York. The names of all other peculiars are shown in bold type and can be identified from the key letters.

The peculiars of St. Leonard's Hospital, York (SLH) and of Beverley (BG) had concurrent jurisdiction with the exchequer court over a number of parishes, ceasing by the mid-16th century. Likewise the jurisdiction of the dean and chapter of York (DC) over a few parishes faded out, although it continued in many others. In such cases where the exchequer court had later jurisdiction, these places are included in the following alphabetical list but are not shown on the maps.

Acklam, (E), LE 36
Acomb (A), **AC** 46
Airmyn (W), SN 96
Aldborough (N), DC 17
Aldborough (W), DC 70
Aldbrough (in Stanwick St. John) (N), **AD** 1
Allerston (N), DY 11
Allerthorpe (E), DY 52
Allerton and Allertonshire (N), **AE** 8
Allerton Mauleverer (W), R 77
Alne (N), **AH** 21
Altofts (W), **AL** 93
Ampleforth (N), **AM** 14
Anderby Steeple (N), R
Anston (W), LE 104
Appleton Wiske (N), R
Arkendale (W), K 76
Arkengarthdale (N), **AR** 4
Askham Bryan (A) **AS** 48
Askrigg (N), R
Asselby (E), HO 56
Austerfield (W), AN 101
Aysgarth (N), R
Balne (W), SN 96
Barlby (E), HO 56
Barlow (W), SE 90
Barmby Marsh (E), HO 56
Barmby Moor (E), DY & **BA** 52
Barnby (E) DY & BA 52
Barnoldswick (W), **BD** 81
Barton (N), R
Batley (W) **BE** 92
Bedale (N), R
Beeford (E), **BF** 43
Beilby (E), DY 52
Beningbrough (N), NO 23
Bentham (W), RW 68
Beverley (E), **BG**

Bielby (E), DY 52
Bilton in Ainsty (A), **BI** 44
Bilton in Holderness (E), BG
Bingley (W), CR 84
Bishop Wilton (E) **BS** 40
Blacktoft (E), HO 56
Blubberhouses (W), K 76
Blyth (W and Notts.), AN 101
Bolton (nr Pocklington) (E), BS 40
Bolton upon Swale (N), R
Castle Bolton (N), R
Boston (Spa) (W), DC 83
Bowes (N), R
Bramham (W), DC 83
Brandesburton (E), BG
Brantingham (E), HO 62
Brayton (W), SE 90
Brignall (N), R
Brompton (N), AE 8
Brotherton (W), DC 95
Bubwith (E), DC
Bugthorpe (E), **BU** 39
Burn (W), SE 90
Burneston (N), R & SLH
Burton Leonard (W), DC 76
Burton Pidsea (E), BG & DC 66
Carlton in Snaith (W), SN 96
Carlton Husthwaite (N), HU 16
Carnaby (E), SLH
Castley (W), K 76
Cattal (W), HS 78
Catterick (N), R
North Cave (E), SLH
South Cave (E), **CA** & SLH 61
Cawood (W), WI 87
Cayton (W), K 76
Chapel le Dale (W), RW 68
Cherry Burton (E), BG
Church Fenton (W), FE 86

Clapham (W), RW 68
Cleasby (N), R
Clint (W), K 76
Coneythorpe (W), K 76
Copgrove (W), R 73
Copmanthorpe (A), DC 49
Cottam (E) LA 34
Cottingley (W), CR 84
Coverham (N), R
Cowick (W), SN 96
East Cowton (N), R
South Cowton (N), R
Crayke (N), CD 19
Croft (N), R
Crossley (W), **CR** 84
Cundall (N), R 17
South Dalton (E), BG
Dalton on Tees (N), DC
Danby Wiske (N), R
Deighton (N) AE 8
Dent (W), RW 68
Dob Cross (W), CC 98
Downholme (N), R
Driffield (E), **DR** 38
Drypool (E), BG
Dukeswick (W), K 76
Dunnington (E), **DU** 51
Dunsforth (W), DC 70
Easby (N), R
Eastrington (E), HO 56
Ebberston (N), DY 11
Ellerburn (N), DY 11
Ellerker (E), HO 62
Elloughton (E), WG 63
Eryholme (N), R
Fangfoss (E), DY 41
Farnham (W), K 76
Fenton (W), **FE** 86
Fewston (W), K 76
Fimber (E), WG 37

Yorkshire, continued
Finghall (N), R
Finningley (W and Notts.) AN 101
Firbeck (W), LE 104
Forcett (N), R
Foston on the Wolds (E), BG
Fridaythorpe (E), **FR** & WG 37
Garsdale (W), RW 68
Gateforth (W), SE 90
Gate Helmsley (N) BG & O 27
Gildingwells (W), LE 104
Gilling (N), R
Gisburn (W), SLH
Givendale (E), DY & **GI** 42
Goathland (N), DY 10
Goldsborough (W), R 77
Goodmanham (E), DC
Goole (W), SN 96
Gowdall (W), SN 96
North Grimston (E), LA 33
Grindal (E), **GR** 32
Grinton (N), R
Hambleton (W), SE 90
Hampsthwaite (W), K 76
Handsworth (W), LE 103
Hardraw (N), R
Harrogate (W), K 76
Hartwith (W), MF 71
Hauxwell (N), R
Haverah Park (W), K 76
Hawes (N), R
Haxby (N), DR & ST 25
Hayton (E), DY 52
Heath (W), WB 94
Heck (W), SN 96
Over Helmsley (N), SLH
Helperby (N), DC 18
Helperthorpe (E), DC 31
Hemingbrough (E), HO 56
Hensall (W), SN 96
Heslington (E), AM 50
Hipswell (N), R
Holme Archiepiscopi (E), **HA** - see Withernwick
Holtby (N), HO 29
Hook (W), SN 96
Hope (in Barningham) (N), AR 4
Hornby (N), DC 9
Hotham (E), SLH
Howden and Howdenshire (E), **HO** 56
Hudswell (N), R
Hunsingore (W), **HS** 78
Husthwaite (N), **HU** 16
Hutton Conyers (N), R
Hutton Magna (N), R
Ingleton (W), RW 68
Kilham (E), DY 35
Killinghall (W), K 76
Kilnwick Percy (E), DY 52

Kirby Hill (N), R 17
Kirby Sigston (N), AE 8
Kirby Wiske (N), R
Kirkby Fleetham (N), R
Kirkby Malzeard (W), MF 69
Kirkby Ravensworth (N), R
Kirkby Wharfe (W), WG 85
Kirk Hammerton (W), R 77
Kirklington (N), R
Knaresborough (W), **K** 76
Langtoft (E), **LA** 34
Great Langton (N), R
Laughton-en-le-Morthen (W), **LE** 104
Laxton (E), HO 56
Leconfield (E), BG
Letwell (W), LE 104
Leven (E), BG
Lindley (W), K 76
Linton on Ouse (N), **LI** 22
Lowthorpe (E), BG
Lunds (N), R
Luttons Ambo (E), DC 31
Lydgate (W), CC 98
Manfield (N), R
Mappleton (E), **MA** 54
Market Weighton (E), WE 53
Marrick (N), R
Marsden (W), **MD** 97
Marske (N), R
Marton cum Grafton (W), R 77
Masham (N) **MF** 13
Meltonby (E), DY 52
Mexborough (W), **MH** 99
Micklefield (W), FE 86
Middleham (N), **MI** 12
Middlesmoor (W), MF 69
Middleton Tyas (N), R
Middleton on the Wolds (E), BG
Millington (E) DY & GI 42
Monk Fryston (W), WI 91
Muker (N), R
Murton (N), O & ST 30
North Newbald (E), **NN** 57
South Newbald (E), NN 57
New Forest (in Kirkby Ravensworth) (N), AR 4
Newton on Ouse (N), **NO** & SLH 23
Newton nr. Pickering (N), DY 10
Nidd (W), R 72
Normanton (W) - see Altofts
Northallerton (N), AE 8
Nunburnholme (E), SLH
Nun Monkton (W), R 77
Osbaldwick (N), **O** & ST 30
Ottringham (E), BG
Great Ouseburn (W), K 74
Little Ouseburn (W), DR 75
Ousefleet (W), SN 96
Pannal (W), K 76

Patrick Brompton (N), R
Patrington (E), BG
Pickering (N), DY 10
Pickhill (N) R & SLH
Plompton (W), K 76
Pocklington (E) DY 52
Pollington (W), SN 96
Upper Poppleton (A), DC 45
Preston in Holderness (E), **PH** 65
Pudsey (W), CR 88
Ravenfield (W), MH 102
Rawcliffe (W), SN 96
Reedness (W), SN 96
Great Ribston (W), HS 78
Riccall (E) **RI** 55
Richmond (N), R
Rigton (W), K 76
Ripley (W), R 72
Rokeby (N), R
Romaldkirk (N), R
Rossington (W), AN 101
West Rounton (N), AE 6
Routh (E), BG
Rufforth (A), SLH
Ruston (E), BG
Saddleworth (in Rochdale, Lancs) (W), CC 98
Salton (N), **SA** 15
Saxton (W), SLH
Scorborough (E), BG
Scruton (N), R
Sedbergh (W), RW 68
Selby (W), **SE** 90
Sherburn in Elmet (W), FE 86
Shipton (E) WE 53
Shiptonthorpe (E), WE 53
Sigglesthorne (E), BG
Silsden (W), **SI** 82
Skelton nr. York (N), AH 24
Skipwith (E), HO 56
Great Smeaton (N), R
Snaith (W), SN 96
Sockburn (N), CD 2
Spennithorpe (N), R
Stainburn (W), K 76
South Stainley (W), K 76
Stalling Busk (N), R
Startforth (N), R
Staveley (W), K & R 76
Stillington (N) **SO** 20
Stockton on the Forest (N), BU 26
Strensall (N), **ST** 25
Swindon (W), K 76
Swinefleet (W), SN 96
West Tanfield (N), R
Temple Newsam (W), **TN** 89
Thornton in Lonsdale (W), RW 68

YORKSHIRE: EAST RIDING
and the CITY and AINSTY of YORK
(now mainly in Humberside; north and west border,
including York, in North Yorkshire)

Since 1858: see Yorkshire, page 57.

Before 1858: The East Riding and the City and
Ainsty of York were wholly in the diocese and
province of York, and, apart from peculiars, in the
jurisdiction of the **Exchequer Court**.
 The records of this and of nearly all the peculiars
are at

The Borthwick Institute, York.

 See page 56 for indexes and records of P.C.Y.,
the Exchequer Court, the Chancery Court, and the
Court of the Dean and Chapter of York (which had
jurisdiction in 14 parishes in York, 2 in the Ainsty
and 5 in the East Riding; see list pages 58-60).
 The list on pages 58-60 shows which parishes lay
in the many peculiars. The initials used as a key to
these are shown in parentheses, right. There are
TS indexes to the wills, admons and invs in all of
these peculiar courts, unless shown otherwise. The
Chancery Court and the Court of the Dean and
Chapter also had jurisdiction in many peculiars,
and these are asterisked.
 Published: *York Clergy Wills 1520-1600* (2 vols.),
ed. Claire Cross, York, 1984, 1989.

Peculiars:
Acomb (AC), 1456-1837.
Ampleforth* (AM), 1528-1827.
Askham Bryan (AS), 1715-1799.
Barnby (Barmby Moor)* (BA), 1610-1729
 thereafter, Pec. of the Dean of York).
Beeford (BF), 1561-1678 (Y.A.S.R.S. 68).
Bilton* (BI), 1591-1849.
Bishop Wilton, 1531-1842 (calendar only).
Bugthorpe* (BU), 1544-1831.
South Cave (CA), 1558-1579 (TS index), 1579-
 1843 (calendar).
Driffield* (DR), 1557-1852.
Dunnington* (DU), 1549-1729 (thereafter see the
 exchequer court).
Fridaythorpe* (FR), 1593-1730 (thereafter see
 prebend of Wetwang).
Givendale* (GI), 1661-1669.
Grindal* (GR), 1623-1629 (thereafter see
 exchequer court).
Holme Archiepiscopi* (HA), 1560-1836.
Howden and Howdenshire (HO), 1521-1857
 (calendar only, 1598-1622).
Langtoft* (LA), 1520-1845.
Laughton-en-le-Morthen* (LE), 1548-1857.
Mappleton* (MA) 1571-1849.
North Newbald* (NN), 1496-1851.
Preston in Holderness* (PH), 1559-1837.
Riccall* (RI), 1549-1833.
Tunstall* (TU), 1557-1838.
(Market) Weighton* (WE), 1502-1857.
Wetwang* (WG), 1559-1850 (see also
 Fridaythorpe).

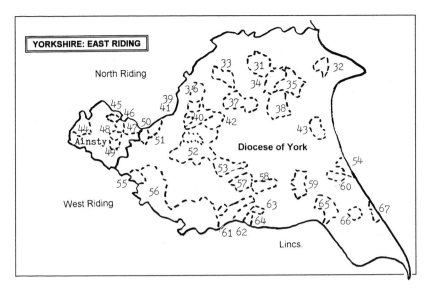

YORKSHIRE: EAST RIDING

North Riding

Ainsty

West Riding

Diocese of York

Lincs.

YORKSHIRE: NORTH RIDING

(now mainly in North Yorkshire, with northern borders in Durham and Cleveland)

Since 1858: see Yorkshire, page 57.

Before 1858: The North Riding of Yorkshire was split between the dioceses of York and Chester, both in the province of York. The eastern half lay in the diocese of York and was, apart from peculiars, in the jurisdiction of the **Exchequer Court**. The records of this, of P.C.Y. and of the **Chancery Court**, are at the *Borthwick Institute, York*, and are described on page 56. Records of the many peculiar courts, also at the *Borthwick Institute*, are detailed right.

The western half of the North Riding was in the **Archdeaconry of Richmond, Eastern Deaneries**, in the diocese of Chester. The records of this court are at

---

Leeds District Archives
(West Yorks. Archives Service), *Leeds.*

The parishes in this jurisdiction (**R**) and in peculiars, are listed on pages 58-60. There is a 19th cent. MS index to wills and admons, c1427-1857; and a card index, wills, admons and invs, 1521-1610, 1711-1750 (and in progress); also printed index, wills and admons, 1471-1616, A-G only (*Northern Genealogist*, vols. **3-5**).

Leeds District Archives also holds indexed records of three North Riding peculiars:

Arkengarthdale (AR) 1698-1812.
Masham (MF) 1581-1857. Calendar and index, incl. surnames of beneficiaries etc published 1994 by *Ripon Historical Society* and *Ripon, Harrogate & District Family History Group.*
Middleham (MI) 1722-1854.

Records of most of the **peculiars** in the North Riding are at the

---

Borthwick Institute, *York*

---

as described on page 60, and the places in them are listed on pages 58-60. The **Court of the Dean and Chapter** had jurisdiction in Helperby and Hornby in the North Riding, and this and the **Chancery Court** had jurisdiction in many peculiars, as asterisked, see page 56.

Dean of York* (DY) (jurisdiction incl. 7 parishes in the North Riding), 1604-1722 (printed, *Y.A.S.R.S.* **73**); 1531-1708, 1722-1857 (TS index).
Aldborough (in Stanwick St. John) (AD), 1610-1700 (*Y.A.S.R.S.* **60**) (in *York Minster Library*).
Alne and Tollerton (AH), 1458-1856.
Ampleforth* (AM), 1528-1827.
Bugthorpe*, 1544-1831.
Howden and Howdenshire (incl. Holtby in the North Riding) (HO), 1521-1857 (calendar 1598-1622 only).
Husthwaite* (HU), 1633-1661 (TS), 1661-1842 (calendar).
Linton on Ouse (LI), 1710-1735.
Newton on Ouse with Beningbrough (NO), 1614-1812.
Osbaldwick* (O), 1549-1827.
Salton* (SA), 1531-1826.
Stillington* (SO), 1515-1843.
Strensall* (ST), 1528-1640 (TS). 1640-1739 (calendar), 1740-1852 (TS).
Warthill* (WD), 1548-1837.
Westerdale (WF) (records now lost). 1550-1575, 1669-1765 (*Y.A.S.R.S.* **74**).

For a map of the North Riding, see page 62.

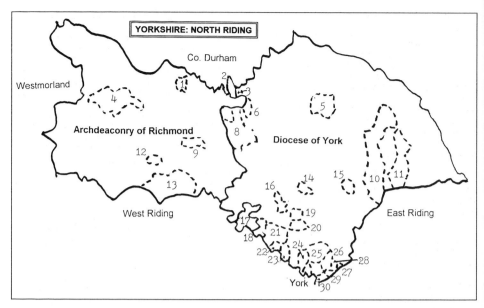

YORKSHIRE: NORTH RIDING

Co. Durham

Westmorland

Archdeaconry of Richmond

Diocese of York

West Riding

East Riding

York

Yorkshire: North Riding, continued

> **Durham University Library (Archives and Special Collections),** *Durham* (see page 25)

also has a few probate records for the North Riding:

Consistory Court of Durham with Bishop of Durham's Peculiars of Crayke and of Allertonshire: jurisdiction incl. Over Dinsdale and Girsby, townships in the parish of Sockburn (mostly in co. Durham); until 1837 the Bishop of Durham's peculiar of Crayke (then in co. Durham but from 1844 in Yorkshire); and until 1846 the bishop of Durham's peculiar of Allertonshire in Yorkshire (containing Birkby, Cowesby, Hutton Bonville, Leake, Nether Silton, North Otterington, Osmotherly and Thornton-le-Street). In main index to Durham probate records.

Peculiar of the Dean and Chapter of Durham in Allerton and Allertonshire (AE) (jurisdiction covered Brompton, Deighton, High Worsall, Kirby Sigston, Northallerton and West Rounton, all in Yorkshire. These places were transferred to York diocese in 1846). Index, wills, admons and invs, **1666-1845**.

YORKSHIRE: WEST RIDING
(now split between West, South and North Yorkshire, with western border areas in Cumbria, Lancashire and Greater Manchester; and the eastern Goole area in Humberside).

Since 1858: see Yorkshire, page 57.

Before 1858: Nearly all the West Riding of Yorkshire lay in the diocese of York and, apart from peculiars, the jurisdiction of the **Exchequer Court**. records of this, and of P.C.Y., are now at the

> *Borthwick Institute, York,*

and are described on page 56.

Records of most West Riding **peculiars** are also at the *Borthwick Institute*, as described on page 60, and the places in them are listed on pages 58-60. The **Court of the Dean and Chapter** had jurisdiction in six West Riding parishes, and this and the **Chancery Court** had jurisdiction in many peculiars, as asterisked, see page 56.

Barnoldswick (BD), 1660-1794 (very few) (printed, *Y.A.S.R.S.* ***118***).

Crossley, Bingley, Cottingley and Pudsey (CR), 1586-1676 (some) *(Northern Genealogist, 1)*; calendar to 1804.

Driffield* (DR), 1557-1852.

Fenton* (FE), 1528-1854.

Laughton en le Morthen* (LE), 1548-1857.

Marsden (MD), 1664-1855 *(Northern Genealogist, 2)* (also calendar from 1655).

Mexborough and Ravenfield* (ME), wills 1662-1740, 1760-1839 (calendar).

Selby (SE), 1555-1857 (calendar from 1681); 1634-1710 (printed abstracts, *Y.A.S.R.S.* ***47***).

Yorkshire: West Riding, continued

Silsden (SI), 1588-1737 *(Northern Genealogist, 1)*, 1737-1809 (calendar).
Snaith (SN), 1568-1857 (calendar).
Temple Newsam (TN), 1612-1701 *(Northern Genealogist, 1*; and *Thoresby Soc. 33)*
Ulleskelf* (U), 1612-1751 (see also prebend of Wetwang).
Wadworth* (WA), 1639-1819 (see also prebend of South Cave, East Riding).
Wetwang* (WG), 1588-1850 (see also prebend of Ulleskelf).
Wistow (WI), 1558-1842.

Leeds District Archives

has records of the **Archdeaconry of Richmond, Eastern Deaneries,** which included all parishes in the deanery of Boroughbridge not in peculiars. Indexes, page 61, places listed on pages 58-60.

Peculiars (and other original wills) at *Leeds Archives Dept.*:

Altofts in Normanton (AL), 1622-1677 (printed, *Northern Genealogist 1*).
Hunsingore (HN), 1607-1839 (MS).
Knaresborough (K), 1640-1857 (*Surtees Soc. 110*; also abstracts, *104*).
Leeds Kirkgate, 1626-1669
Masham (MF) 1581-1857. Calendar and index, incl. surnames of beneficiaries etc published 1994 by *Ripon Historical Society* and *Ripon, Harrogate & District Family History Group.*
Warmfield with Heath (WB), 1613-1695 *(Northern Genealogist, 1*, p. 129).
Whitkirk, 1673-1773.

Lancashire Record Office, Preston

has records of the **Western Deaneries of the Archdeaconry of Richmond.** These include four extreme north-west parishes in the deanery of Lonsdale (listed on pages 58-60). Wills and admons, 1457-1720 (19th cent calendar), 1720-1857 (calendar). Non-Lancashire parishes were omitted from *L&CRS* printed indexes.

Also at the *Lancashire R.O.* are records of the **Consistory Court of Chester,** whose jurisdiction covered the West Riding chapelries of Whitewell (in Whalley) and Saddleworth (in Rochdale), page 33.

The West Riding parishes of Rossington and parts of the Notts parishes of Blyth and Finningley in the West Riding were in the **Archdeaconry of Nottingham,** records partly at *Nottinghamshire Record Office*, page 41.

West Riding Registry of Deeds (founded 1704, now part of the *West Yorkshire Record Office*), *Wakefield,*

has registered copies of many West Riding wills. These are indexed 1704-1879, forming an important complementary source to the normal probate collections. The usefulness of these registered wills varies considerably. Some are very full summaries, others are only brief extracts.

Bradford Central Library has records of the **Manor of Batley,** 1651-1753 *(Y.A.S.R.S. 74).*

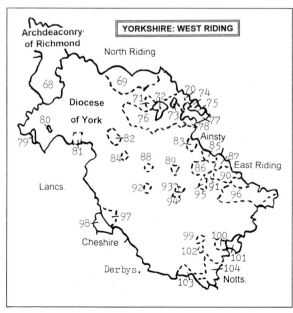

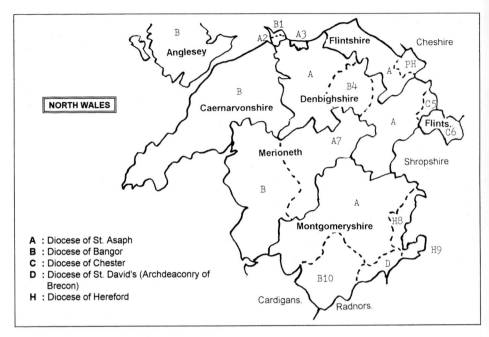

A : Diocese of St. Asaph
B : Diocese of Bangor
C : Diocese of Chester
D : Diocese of St. David's (Archdeaconry of Brecon)
H : Diocese of Hereford

Caernarvonshire
Llandudno **B1**; Eglwys-Rhos **A2**; Llangystennin **A2**; Llysfaen **A3**;

Denbighshire (B4)
Clocaenog, Derwen, Efenechtid, Gyffylliog, Llanbedr, Dyffryn Clwyd, Llandyrnog, Llanelidan, Llanfair Dyffryn Clwyd, Llanfywrog, Llangwyfan, Llangynhafal, Llanhychan, Llanrhaeadr-yng-Nghinmeirch, Llan-rhudd, Llanynys, Ruthin; Holt **C5**.

Flintshire
Peculiar of Hawarden (**PH**);
Southern Detachment (**C6**):
Bangor Iscoed, Hanmer, Overton, Threapwood, Worthenbury.

Merionethshire (A7)
Betws Gwerful Goch, Corwen, Gwyddelwern, Llandderfel, Llandrillo, Llanfor, Llangar, Llangywer, Llansanffraid Glyndyfrdwy, Llanymawddwy, Llanuwchllyn, Llanycil, Mallwyd.

Montgomeryshire
Alberbury (partly Salop) **H8**; Buttington **H8**; Carno **B10**; Churchstoke **H9**; Forden **H8**; Hyssington **H9**; Kerry (Ceri) **D**; Llandinam **B10**; Llangurig **B10**; Llanidloes **B10**; Llanwynog **B10**; Mainstone (partly Salop) **H9**; Mochdre **D**; Montgomery **H8**; Penstrowed **B10**; Snead **H9**; Trefeglwys **B10**; Worthen (partly Salop) **H8**.

For the Episcopal Consistory Court of Hereford (with jurisdiction over nine parishes in Montgomeryshire) see *Hereford Record Office*, page 19.

NORTH WALES

ANGLESEY, CAERNARVONSHIRE, DENBIGHSHIRE, FLINTSHIRE, MERIONETHSHIRE, MONTGOMERYSHIRE

Since 1858: Probate records for England and Wales are at the *Principal Registry of the Family Division, Somerset House, Strand, London WC2R 1LP*. Indexes to these are held locally at *Aberystwyth, Caernarfon, Chester* and *Ruthin* - see page 11 for locations and finishing dates, and for copies elsewhere.

Registered copy wills from 1858 for all Welsh counties except Montgomeryshire are deposited at the *National Library of Wales*. Those proved at St. Asaph (Denbighs, Flint, Merioneth) are indexed 1860-61, 1865-1923 and those at Bangor (Anglesey, Caernarvonshire) are indexed 1858-1941. Those for Montgomeryshire were proved at Shrewsbury and are deposited at the *Shropshire Record Office*.

Original wills proved at Bangor from 1858 and St. Asaph, 1858-1928, are at the *Bangor Probate Sub-Registry, Bangor*.

North Wales, continued

Before 1858: These six counties were in the province of Canterbury (P.C.C., page 12) and mainly in the diocese of Bangor and/or St. Asaph; but with a very few parishes also in the diocese of Chester (for which see also P.C.Y., page 56), Hereford and St. David's.
There is an index (on microfilm) of Welsh wills in PCC for most of the 18th century, arranged by county, at the *N.L.W.* [film 294].
Anglesey was wholly in Bangor.
Caernarvonshire was wholly in Bangor except for three parishes in St. Asaph.
Denbighshire was mainly in St. Asaph; with 16 central parishes in Bangor, and 1 parish in Chester.
Flintshire was mainly in St. Asaph; with the 5 parishes in the southern detachment, and the peculiar of Hawarden, in Chester (see also P.C.Y.).
Merionethshire was in Bangor (22 parishes) and St. Asaph (13 parishes).
Montgomeryshire was mainly in St. Asaph, with seven southern parishes in Bangor, two parishes in the archdeaconry of Brecon (diocese of St. David's) and nine parishes or parts of parishes in the episcopal consistory of Hereford.
Except for Hereford, the records of all these courts are at the

---
National Library of Wales, Aberystwyth.

Prior application should be made for a readers' ticket. A brief guide, *Probate Records in the National Library of Wales*, 1990, is available.
1. **Consistory Court of Bangor**, wills, admons and invs, **1635-1700** (index published by N.L.W., 1980); **1700-1857** (MS calendar).
2. **Consistory Court of St. Asaph**, reg. copy wills **1565-1623**, **1637-1648**; orig. wills, admons, invs **1583-84**, **1606**, **1609**, **1612**, **1623**, **1625**, **1627**, **1633-34**, **1636**, **1638-1647** (revised index in progress); wills, admons, invs **1660-1700** (card index in progress for publication); **1660-1729** (calendar, alphabetical by Christian name), **1729-1820** (card index, surnames), **1821-1857** (calendar, surnames).
3. **Consistory Court of Chester** (jurisdiction, Holt, Denbighs., and the southern detachment of Flint. Records relating to these Welsh parishes have been separated from those for the remaining, English, part of the diocese).
Wills, admons and invs, 1546-1837 (*Lancashire & Cheshire Record Society*, see page 19).
4. **Archdeaconry of Brecon** (Kerry and Mochdre in Montgomeryshire - see page 66).
5. **Peculiar Court of Hawarden**. Wills, admons and invs, **1554-1800** (printed index, *Flintshire Hist. Soc. vol. 4, pt. 2*); **1801-1857** (unpublished index).

SOUTH WALES

BRECKNOCK, CARDIGAN, CARMARTHEN, GLAMORGAN, MONMOUTH, PEMBROKE, RADNOR

Since 1858: Probate records for England and Wales are at the *Principal Registry of the Family Division, Somerset House, Strand, London WC2R 1LP*. Indexes to these (to 1928) are held locally at the *Glamorgan Record Office, Cardiff*, and at *Dyfed Archives Office, Carmarthen;* for other copies, see page 11.
Registered copy wills from 1858 for all these counties are deposited at the *National Library of Wales*. Those proved at Llandaff (Monmouth and Glamorgan, except Gower) are indexed to 1905; at Carmarthen (Cardigan, Carmarthen, Pembroke and Gower) to 1941 and at Hereford (Radnor and Brecknock) to 1928.

Before 1858: These seven counties were in the province of Canterbury (for P.C.C. see page 12) and almost entirely in the dioceses of St. David's and Llandaff, except for eight parishes in the diocese of Hereford. Within the diocese of St. David's the archdeaconry of Brecon had its own independent consistory court.
There is an index (on microfilm) of Welsh wills in P.C.C. for most of the 18th century, arranged by county, at the *N.L.W.* [film 294].
Carmarthen, **Cardigan** and **Pembroke** (archdeaconry of St. David's) were wholly in the diocese of St. David's and the jurisdiction of its consistory court.
Brecknock was wholly and **Radnor** mainly in the archdeaconry of Brecon and the jurisdiction of its consistory court; six Radnorshire parishes were in the diocese of Hereford and the jurisdiction of the episcopal consistory of Hereford.
Glamorgan was mainly and **Monmouth** almost entirely in the diocese of Llandaff; but 23 parishes in the Gower peninsular in Glamorgan were in the diocese and consistory of St. David's (archdeaconry of Carmarthen); in Monmouth three parishes were in the archdeaconry of Brecon and two in the diocese and consistory of Hereford.

Except for Hereford, the records of all these courts are at the

---
National Library of Wales, Aberystwyth.

Prior application should be made for a readers' ticket. A brief guide, *Probate Records in the National Library of Wales*, 1990, is available.

1. **Episcopal Consistory Court of St. David's: Archdeaconry of Cardigan**
wills, admons and invs **1594-1747** (lists, chronological), admons **1700-1740** (index), wills and admons, 1746-1857 (calendar). M'fiche: Testators index to abstrs of original wills 1564-1750, St David's diocese; index by parish, all St David's diocese, Episcopal Consistory Court (excl. archdeaconries).

South Wales, continued

Archdeaconry of Carmarthen, wills, admons and invs **1594-1816** (chronological lists; **1780-1816** card index in preparation); **1817-36** (card index; separate card index to stray co. Cardigan entries); **1837-57** (calendar).
Archdeaconry of St. David's, wills, admons and invs, **1594-1629, 1649-1653, 1700-1747** (chronological lists); admons **1700-1740** (index); wills, admons and invs **1746-1857** (calendar).
2. **Consistory Court of the Archdeaconry of Brecon,** wills **1570-1589, 1609-1658,** index published by N.L.W., 1989; wills, admons and invs **1660-77,** wills **1694-1703** (calendars), wills, admons and invs **1733-1782** (endorsed 'not reliable'), **1783-1857** (calendar); **1678-1785** (chronological lists). TS index to pre-1660.
3. **Consistory Court of Llandaff,** wills, admons and invs **1575-1857** (calendar).

For the **Episcopal Consistory Court of Hereford** (with jurisdiction over two parishes in Monmouth and six in Radnor) see *Hereford Record Office,* page 29.

Glamorgan (D5)
Bishopston, Cheriton, Ilston, Knelston, Llanddewi, LLandeilo Tal-y-Bont, Llangennith, Llan-giwg, LLangyfelach, Llanmadog, LLanrhidian, LLansamlet, Loughor, Nicholaston, Oxwich, Oystermouth, Penmaen, Pennard, Penrice, Port Einon, Reynoldston, Rhosili, Swansea.

Monmouth
Cwmyoy **B3,** Dixton Newton **H4;** LLanthony **B3;** Monmouth **H4;** Oldcastle **B3.**

Radnor
Discoed **H1;** Knighton **H1;** Michaelchurch-on-Arrow **H2;** Norton **H1;** Presteigne **H1;** Old and New Radnor **H1.**

B : Archdeaconry of Brecon
     (Diocese of St. David's)
D : Diocese of St. David's
H : Diocese of Hereford
L : Diocese of Llandaff

SOUTH WALES

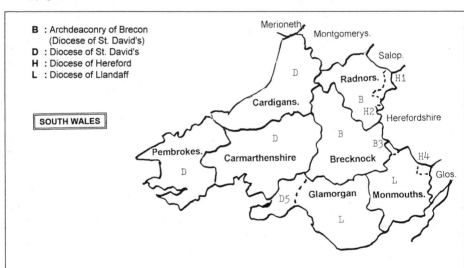

ISLE OF MAN

Since 1847: Probate records from the two courts which had joint jurisdiction in the island (see below) are at the *Manx Museum* (see below) to 1910 and at the *Deeds and Probate Registry* post-1910. From 1874 the Consistory Court had sole jurisdiction, and from 1885 testamentary business has been in the High Court of Justice. If the deceased lived or had property outside the island, then see also the Principal Registry, page 11.

Before 1847: The Isle of Man was in the province of York and the diocese of Sodor and Man.
  Apart from P.C.Y. (page 56) and P.C.C. (page 12) all probate records for the island are at the

Manx Museum Library, Douglas.

These comprise the **Consistory Court of Sodor and Man**, from 1600 (index starts in 1659) and the **Archdeaconry Court of the Isle of Man**, from 1631 (indexed).
  The two courts both had jurisdiction throughout the island, alternating for parts of the year, so it is necessary always to search both.

CHANNEL ISLANDS
JERSEY

Probate matters were subject to the ecclesiastical court of the **Dean of Jersey** until as recently as 1949. The records are with the

Judicial Greffe, Royal Court, Jersey

and comprise: wills **1660-1964** (indexed), admons **1848-1964** (calendars).

GUERNSEY

Grants of Representation are still issued by the

Ecclesiastical Court of the Bailiwick of Guernsey, *Bureau des Connetables*, *St. Peter Port.*

The records, wills and admons (incl. Alderney, Sark, Herm and Jethou), date from 1660, and are indexed.
  Wills devising real estate (Guernsey only), from 1841 only, are to be found in the

Royal Court of Guernsey, *The Greffe, Royal Court, Guernsey.*

In cases where the deceased had property in England or Wales, see also P.C.C. (page 12). The Channel Islands were in the diocese of Winchester, but have always been administered separately.

SCOTLAND

See Scottish Record Office Leaflet No. **19**, *Indexes in the Historical Search Room to Deeds, Sasines and Testamentary Records*, 1990.

Since 1876: An annual consolidated calendar of confirmations has been prepared and, until recent years, printed. This can be examined at the

Scottish Record Office,
HM General Register House, Edinburgh

in the *Historical Search Room* (to 1935; full set in the *Legal Search Room;* also probably available in some local archives and libraries). Most non-current Sheriff court testamentary records are now deposited in the *Scottish Record Office,* unless still retained by the relevant sheriff clerk. Sheriffdoms, at first generally coinciding with counties, have now often been merged into larger groupings. The *Scottish Law Directory* lists the sheriff court districts and the parishes in each.

Since 1823: In this year the old probate jurisdictions of commissariots (see below) were abolished and replaced by sheriffdoms, at that time generally the same as the counties, though from the start Perthshire and Argyll were each split into two districts, and so was Angus from 1832.

There are consolidated printed indexes to *Personal Estates of Defuncts* arranged in three groups: the Lothians, 1827-1865; Argyll, Bute, Dumbarton, Lanark and Renfrew, 1846-1865; and the remainder of Scotland, 1846-1867.

Most of the Sheriff Court commissary records are kept in separate series for confirmations, wills, and inventories. The *Scottish Record Office* should be consulted on whether the probate records of the relevant sheriff court have been retained locally or deposited. Most of the following indexes (MS unless shown as TS) are to inventories:

Aberdeen, 1824-1875.
Alloa, 1824-1877.
Ayr, 1824-46, 1867-75.
Banff, 1824-1916.
Cupar, 1823-1892, TS.
Dingwall, 1824-1900, TS.
Dornoch, 1851-1885.
Dumbarton, 1824-1876.
Dumfries, 1827-1876.
Dunblane, 1824-1900, TS.
Dundee, 1832-1845, TS; 1832-1876.
Dunoon, 1815-1900, TS.
Duns, 1823-1876.
Edinburgh, 1808-1901; Probates re-sealed ('furth of Scotland'), TS.
Elgin, 1824-1876.
Forfar, 1824-1875.
Glasgow, 1824-1875.
Haddington, 1830-1898, TS.
Hamilton, 1888-1899.
Inveraray *see* Dunoon.

Inverness, 1825-1876.
Jedburgh, 1827-1912.
Kinross, 1847-1881.
Kirkcudbright, 1824-1876.
Linlithgow, 1831-1897, TS.
Nairn, 1839-1881.
Paisley, 1824-1899, TS.
Peebles, 1814-1878.
Perth, 1824-1900, TS.
Rothesay, 1824-1876.
Selkirk, 1824-1876.
Stirling, 1809-1900.
Stonehaven, 1824-1877.
Stornoway, 1827-1840, TS.
Wick, 1829-1876.
Wigtown, 1838-1879.

Before 1823: All pre-1823 records are deposited at the

Scottish Record Office, *Edinburgh.*

Until 1823 the various testamentary jurisdictions in Scotland were called 'commissariots', and the areas covered were based on the medieval dioceses, although the bishops' authority had been abolished in 1560. The principal commissary court, in many respects similar to P.C.C. in England, was that of Edinburgh, and, like that, should always be consulted in addition to local courts.

For the period 1801-1823 there are separate TS indexes at the *S.R.O.* for the commissariots of Edinburgh (to 1829), Glasgow, Peebles (to 1827) and St. Andrews, and a consolidated TS index to the remaining commissariots throughout Scotland.

Indexes to all surviving testaments before 1801 have been published by the *Scottish Record Society (SRS).*

Commissariot of Edinburgh (jurisdiction over persons without fixed domicile or dying 'furth of Scotland'; locally in the Lothians until 1830.
Testaments, **1514-1800** (*SRS 1-3,* also *BRS 16,* **1514-1600**).

Counties (numbers key to map), commissariot jurisdiction, starting dates of testaments, and *SRS* index volumes.

Aberdeen (10) and **Banff** (9): Mainly Aberdeen, **1715** *(SRS 6).*
Angus (or Forfarshire) (14) and **Kincardineshire:** Intermingled, St. Andrews, **1549** *(SRS 8);* Brechin, **1576** *(SRS 13).*
Argyll: Mainland (16), Argyll, **1674** *(SRS 9);* The Islands (15) **1661** *(SRS 11).*
Ayr (34), **Dunbarton** (23), and **Renfrew** (28): Glasgow, **1547** *(SRS 7).*
Banff (9) - see with Aberdeen.
Berwick (32): Lauder, **1561** *(SRS 18).*
Bute (27): The Isles, **1661** *(SRS 11).*
Caithness (1) and **Sutherland** (2): Caithness, **1661-1664** *(SRS 10).*
Clackmannan (22) - see with Stirling.

Scotland, continued

Cromarty - see Ross.
Dumfries (39): Dumfries, **1624** *(SRS 14)*.
Dunbarton (23) - see with Ayr.
East Lothian (Haddington) (31) - see with
  Edinburgh, above.
Edinburgh (Midlothian) (30) - see above.
Elgin (8) - see Moray.
Fife (2) and **Kinross** (20): mainly St. Andrews,
  1549 *(SRS 8)*.
Forfar (14) - see Angus
Haddington (East Lothian) (31) - see with
  Edinburgh, top.
Inverness (11): Mainland mainly Inverness, **1630**
  (SRS 4 and *BRS 20)*. The Isles (6) - see Argyll.
Kincardine (12 and 13) - see with Angus.
Kinross (20) - see with Fife.
Kirkcudbright (40): mainly Kirkcudbright **1663**
  (SRS 17).
Lanark: Glasgow, and Hamilton and Campsie,
  intermingled, north-west half of county (29).
  Glasgow, **1547** *(SRS 7)*; Hamilton, **1564** *(SRS 5*
  and *BRS 20)*. The south-east part (35) in Lanark,
  1595 *(SRS 18)*.
Linlithgow (West Lothian) (26) - see with
  Edinburgh, above.
Midlothian (Edinburgh) (30) - see above.
Moray (Elgin) (8) and **Nairn** (7): Moray, **1684** *(SRS*
  20).
Orkney and **Shetland:** Orkney, **1573-1615** *(SRS*
  6), **1611-1684** *(SRS 21)* (Orkney);
  1611-1649 (Shetland) *(SRS 21)*.
Peebles (36), **Roxburgh** (38) and **Selkirk** (37):
  Peebles, **1681** *(SRS 12)*.
Perth: northern part in Dunkeld (1/), **1682** *(SRS*
  16); southern part in Dunblane (18), **1539** *(SRS*
  15); populous south-west parishes in St. Andrews
  (19) **1549** *(SRS 8)*.
Renfrew (28) - see with Ayr.
Ross and Cromarty (5): Ross, no early records.
Roxburgh (38) and Selkirk (37) - see with Peebles.
Shetland - see with Orkney.
Stirling and **Clackmannan:** mainly in Stirling (25),
  1607 *(SRS 22)*; but see also Glasgow.
Sutherland (2) - see with Caithness.
West Lothian (Linlithgow) 26) - see with Edinburgh,
  top.
Wigtown (41): Wigtown, **1700** *(SRS 23)*.

For names of parishes in various jurisdictions
(when a county is not entirely in one commissariot),
see the relevant *SRS* volumes or *Wills and Where
to Find Them*.

IRELAND

Since 1858: As in England, at this date probate matters were transferred from the ecclesiastical authorities to civil jurisdiction. The *Principal Registry* at *Dublin* also acted as a district registry for the Dublin area, and there were 11 separate district registries.

In 1922 the Four Courts in Dublin including the *Public Record Office of Ireland (P.R.O.I.)* was gutted, and the Principal Registry records to 1903, and original wills from district registries, were lost. Fortunately the will books had remained in the district registries, though these do not contain copies of all wills proved. The most serious loss is for the jurisdiction of the Principal Registry, the counties of Dublin, Kildare, Wicklow, Meath and part of King's County or Offaly.

During the 1920s the *P.R.O.I.* was rebuilt, and a parallel *Public Record Office of Northern Ireland (P.R.O.N.I.)* was established in Belfast. In 1988 *P.R.O.I.* was renamed the *National Archives of Ireland (N.A.I.)*, and in 1992 the headquarters of the *N.A.I.* moved to *Bishop Street* in *Dublin*. The surviving records are now split between Dublin and Belfast. *P.R.O.N.I.* holds records of the district registries of Armagh, Belfast and Londonderry, which include most of the 1858-1922 records of Cos. Louth, Monaghan and Donegal in the Irish Republic. Records of the Principal Registry and the remaining district registries are all now at *N.A.I.* or the appropriate registry (each registry transfers its wills to the *N.A.I.* 20 years after their date of probate). Wills proved in Northern Ireland since 1922 are held in *P.R.O.N.I.* or appropriate registry.

As in England and Wales a General Index of Grants was published annually from 1858. Sets survive in *N.A.I.*, in *P.R.O.N.I.*, and at all district registries. So far as is known there is no set in England.

See also printed indexes for England and Wales, which include many Irish wills and admons - note that for 1858-1876 these are in a separate section following the letter 'Z'; and also see the Scottish Commissary Court.

Before 1858: Ireland was subject to the over-riding jurisdiction of the archbishop of Armagh, and within his province there were some 28 dioceses with the normal consistory courts and at least two peculiars. There were no archdeaconry courts. Virtually all the records of these courts were destroyed in 1922.

All the original manuscript calendars from the Diocesan Courts survived the fire, and a number of printed calendars or indexes have been published; the latter can be found in libraries in England. In particular *N.A.I.* has consolidated indexes of wills and admons from all Irish courts from October 1829 to 1879, and abstracts to 1839, originating in the Inland Revenue Office.

The surviving MS calendars are divided between *N.A.I.* and *P.R.O.N.I.*

Prerogative Court of the Archbishop of Armagh, wills 1536-1810 (printed); 1811-1857; invs 1668-1857; admons 1595-1802.

Counties and the main consistory court jurisdictions in which they lay:

Antrim: Mainly in Connor. Wills and admons, 1661-1857. Printed index to surviving records, 1818-1820, 1853-1857.

Armagh: Mainly in Armagh. Wills 1677-1857 (M-Y); 1687-1838 (C19 copy, *P.R.O.N.I.*); admons 1600-1857.

Carlow: in Leighlin. Wills 1652-1800 *(Phillimore's Irish Wills 1)*; admons 1694-1845 (*The Irish Ancestor*, 1972).

Cavan: Mainly in Kilmore. Wills 1701-1857 (printed); admons 1701-1857.

Clare: Mainly in Killaloe and Kilfenora. Wills 1653-1800 *(Irish Wills 3)*; admons 1704-1857.

Cork: Mainly in Cloyne. Wills 1621-1800 *(Irish Wills 2)*, 1801-1857 (damaged), 1808-1838 (C19 copy), admons 1630-1857. And in Cork and Ross. Wills 1548-1800 *(Irish Wills 2)*, 1801-1857, admons 1612-1857.

Donegal: Mainly in Raphoe. Wills 1684-1857 *(Irish Wills 5)*; admons 1684-1857.

Down: Mainly in Down and Dromore, and the peculiar of Newry and Mourne. Wills, Dromore 1678-1857; Newry and Mourne 1727-1857 *(Irish Wills 4)*; to surviving wills, Down 1850-1857 (printed). Down, wills, 1681-1856, admons 1684-1857; Dromore, wills 1801-1857 (damaged), admons 1749-1857; Newry and Mourne, admons 1811-1845 (*Irish Ancestor, No.1*, 1969, pp. 41-42).

Dublin: In Dublin. Wills 1638-1857 (printed), admons 1697-1845

Fermanagh: Mainly in Clogher. Wills and admons 1660-1857.

Galway: Mainly in Clonfert and Kilmacduagh. Wills 1665-1857, admons 1778-1857 (ptd. *Irish Ancestor*, 1970, 1974; also 1664-1838, with additional information from Betham's copy, ed. P. Smythe-Wood, 1977); and Tuam, admons 1692-1857.

Kerry: In Ardfert and Aghadoe. Wills, 1690-1800 *(Irish Wills 3)*, 1801-1857, admons 1738-1837.

Kildare: Partly in Dublin (for which see co. Dublin) and partly in Kildare. Wills 1661-1800 (*Irish Wills 1*; and in *Jnl. of co. Kildare Arch. Soc. vol. 4, no. 6*), admons 1770-1848 (*Jnl. K.A.S. 5, 3*).

Kilkenny: Mainly Ossory. Wills, 1536-1800 *(Irish Wills 1)*, admons 1845-1857 (printed).

King's County (Offaly): Mainly in Kildare (see co. Kildare) and Killaloe and Kilfenora (see co. Clare).

Leitrim: Mainly in Kilmore (see co. Cavan) and partly in Ardagh (see co. Longford).

Limerick: Mainly in Limerick. Wills 1615-1857 *(Irish Wills 3)*, 1801-1857, admons 1737-1837. And Cashel and Emly, wills 1618-1800 *(Irish Wills 3)*, 1801-1857, admons 1644-1857.

Londonderry: Mainly in Derry. Wills 1612-1857 *(Irish Wills 5)*, admons 1698-1857.

Longford: Mainly in Ardagh. Wills 1695-1857 *(Irish Ancestor, 1971)*; admons 1697-1850.

Louth: Mainly in Armagh (see co. Armagh).

Mayo: In Killala and Achonry. Wills 1698-1838 (from C19 copy), 1839-1857 (fragments only) *(The Irish Genealogist vol. 3, no 12)*; admons 1738-1837 *(Irish Ancestor 7, 1, 1975, pp.55-61)*; and in Tuam, admons 1692-1857.

Meath: Mainly in Meath. Wills 1635-1838, admons 1663-1857.

Monaghan: In Clogher (see co. Fermanagh).

Queen's County (Leix): Mainly in Leighlin (see co. Carlow) and Ossory (see co. Kilkenny).

Roscommon: Mainly in Elphin. Wills 1669-1838, admons 1726-1857.

Sligo: Mainly in Killala and Achonry (see co. Mayo) and Elphin (see co. Roscommon).

Tipperary: Mainly in Cashel and Emly (see co. Limerick) and Killaloe and Kilfenora (see co. Clare).

Tyrone: Mainly in Derry (see co. Londonderry) and Armagh (see co. Armagh).

Waterford: In Waterford and Lismore, with peculiar of the dean of Lismore. Wills 1645-1800 *(Irish Wills 3)*, 1801-1838, admons 1661-1857 (peculiar of Lismore 1766-1846 only).

Westmeath: Mainly in Meath. Wills 1635-1838, admons 1663-1857. Also Ardagh (see co. Longford).

Wexford: Mainly in Ferns. Wills 1601-1800 *(Irish Wills 1)*, 1801-1857 (fragments), admons 1765-1833, grants of probate and admon 1847-1857. Also Dublin (see co. Dublin).

Wicklow: Mainly in Dublin (see co. Dublin). Also Ferns (see co. Wexford) and Leighlin (see co. Carlow).

Unlike English, Welsh and Scottish counties, those in Ireland rarely coincided exactly with probate jurisdictions. For more precise information,

see *Wills and Where to Find Them*. This also cites sources for collections of surviving probate records.

N.A.I. and *P.R.O.N.I.* embarked on a policy of recovering probate copies, office copies, and privately made abstracts of wills from all possible sources, mainly solicitors' offices and genealogists' notes. About one third of all lost wills may have been recovered. Anyone finding a MS text or abstract of a pre-1922 Irish will should notify *N.A.I.* or *P.R.O.N.I.*

Many testators also had property in England and Wales, and therefore may appear in P.C.C. (page 12) or P.C.Y. (page 56). Estate Duty Office will abstracts (mainly from P.C.C) from 1821 to 1857 (and indexes from 1812) are at *P.R.O.N.I.*

It is always worth looking for an Irish will of any date in the appropriate office in London and for the English researcher this may save enquiry in Ireland.

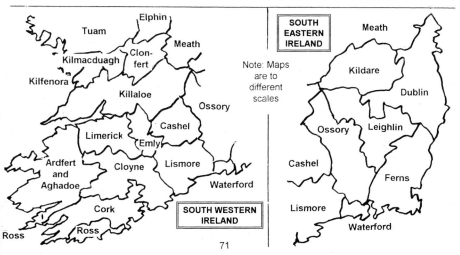

Note: Maps are to different scales